I'D RATHER DO IT MYSELF

FROM MICROMANAGEMENT TO LEADERSHIP

VALERIE DELFORGE

I'd Rather Do It Myself

Copyright © Valerie Delforge, 2023

First Edition

ISBN (paperback) [978-1-914447-92-1]

ISBN (ebook) [978-1-914447-93-8]

All rights reserved. No part of this book may be reproduced in any form, including photocopying and recording, without permission in writing from the publisher, except for brief quotes in review or reference.

This book contains information for entertainment purposes only and should not be used as a substitute for professional medical advice. It is always advisable to consult a medical professional.

Although every effort has been made to ensure the accuracy of the information in this book, no responsibility is assumed for any loss, damage, or disruption caused by errors or omissions, and no liability is assumed for any damages caused by its use.

The views expressed in this book are those of the author alone and do not reflect those of TGH International Ltd..

This book is a work of creative nonfiction, however, certain elements may have been fictionalised in varying degrees for various purposes to suit the narrative.

Prepared by TGH International Ltd.

www.TGHBooks.com

ACKNOWLEDGMENTS

This book is dedicated to all who have supported me throughout my journey, such as my members, past, present, and future, and my amazing team at The Delforge Group®. Also, my loving daughters who have seen me dedicating my time to supporting others and have always understood my work ethos.

FOREWORD

I met Valerie back in 2015 when I reached out to her as a business coach for my own salon at the time. I was at a point in the business where I wasn't sure where to take it. I was experiencing a few problems with the team and how to lead them, and I also wanted to branch out into the skincare side of the business.

My draw to Valerie initially was her 1-1 approach. I had experienced a few coaches prior to this who seemed to give me an off-the-shelf workbook to work through, which apparently would be the answer, but that was so far from what I needed. Valerie had that 1-1 approach and was always there, not just at the sessions but in between. She was my sounding block, my trusted ear, and my personal advisor and mentor.

She helped me to realize my vision at the time, to rebrand and to grow. She showed me how to strategize this and move forward with it. In the meantime, she supported my leadership of the team and planned my step back from the business so that I could focus on my ideas.

I went on to become a multi-award-winning salon and skincare clinic owner, and the rebrand to AMY GORDON was a huge success. The skincare clinic grew, and I expanded into the building next door, and my confidence, ability, and focus became second to none.

When the pandemic hit, I reconnected with Valerie as my passion to help other business owners and empower them to feel the same about their business as I did became apparent. With my knowledge as an owner of a successful and well-established business myself, I felt it was the right time. We joined forces with our combined knowledge, and I haven't looked back since.

I meet a lot of micro-managers along the way who most certainly, if not before the pandemic, feel a loss of control of their business and the know-how of where to start to get back on top. I feel this book will give that insight with a no-nonsense, honest reflection on why and how this happens and how to work towards making those changes and feeling back in control.

Amy Gordon

Director & Business Coach | The Delforge Group©

CONTENTS

Preface   xi

PART I
DEFINING MICROMANAGEMENT

1. WHAT IS MICROMANAGEMENT?   3
   The Definition of Micro-Management   3
   Score your Micro-Management   45

2. WHY DO WE MICROMANAGE?   51
   The Trust Issue   57
   Time Is Not On My Side   61
   Building Blocks   63
   Habits   65

3. THE CONSEQUENCES OF MICROMANAGEMENT   71
   The Work-Life Balance   71
   The Flossy Syndrome   72
   The Team   75
   It's Lonely At The Top   77
   No Growth Allowed   77

PART II
THE SOLUTIONS TO MICROMANAGEMENT

4. LEADERSHIP IN AN OPERATIONAL BUSINESS   83
   Six Leadership Styles   83
   The Soft Skills of Leadership and What Are They For?   118
   The Most Impactful Soft Skills   132

12 Time Management Principles	148
My Time Management Update	185
Learn to Delegate Efficiently	221
The Key Soft Skills Since the Pandemic	228
5. BUILDING TRUST	**243**
Operational Road Map	243
Structure	307
Standard Operating Procedure (SOP) Manual	310
Outsourcing	314
Letting Go of the Past	314
6. SEEING THE BIGGER PICTURE	**319**
A Clear Vision	319
Unlock the Blockages	324
The Systematic Approach	329
Making the Business Work For You	334
Work-Life Wellness	335
7. LEAD THE WAY	**339**
Your Leadership Plan	339
Individual Development Plan & Staff Wellness Formula	345
It's All About Follow-Ups	349
The Leader Inside You - A Recap of What's Next	351

EPILOGUE

1. FINAL REFLECTIONS	359
About the Author	367

PREFACE

I have had my fair share of micro-managers, whether they were direct bosses, colleagues, or clients who joined my coaching programmes. Some of them know they could be working differently but somehow are unable to even contemplate a new style of management, and some of them are simply that way inclined, not even knowing they are behaving that way. If you have picked up this book, then you are on the way to learning about leadership and are ready to take the first step towards the liberation of your workload and growing the business like never before. If someone offered you this book, then it's a hint that something needs to change. For the ones who are simply difficult to work with, then it's a different book altogether, but either way, coaching would be one of the solutions, which is why I love 1-to-1 coaching to personalize the support needed.

They all have, however, the same trait: brilliant at what they do, capable of achieving more than you would think (and we all wonder how with everything they handle!!), and very determined to carry through every task as they believe every single one of them is all very important and no one else can do it better anyhow.

They also have another trait, which we will discuss throughout this book, and that is the one of control. They have an overwhelming feeling of having to control everything, and this keeps them going... But for how long? Will this style of management be detrimental in the long run? Can they achieve a work-life balance without constantly feeling guilty that they should have done this, could have done that, and didn't do this and that? Can they even trust the systems in place to grow better?

A micro-manager will want to oversee every single detail of the operation, and any changes to their overstretched routine add to their ever-expanding to-do list, but that's ok because, you know what? In their mind, it's the "I'd rather do it myself" attitude.

When starting this process shared with you in this book, you will find that every decision becomes a constant battle. You will analyze the outcome in depth, and that's great; it means you are ready to work differently. But of course, the danger is that you go back to your way of working; it's just easier that way.

It takes 66 days to form a new habit. Get yourself a diary, circle the date after 66 days, and stick to your routine until then. If you fail between, start again. If you have a couple of mad weeks, go back to the system. Whatever happens, keep focused and revisit the book at any point to help you with the tools.

This book is dedicated to the micro-managers that I am helping by overcoming their challenges and seeing their workload differently. It is also aimed at those who want to start learning about leadership to grow on a personal and business level to navigate the challenges that life throws at them.

When I started this book, I was working with a brilliant UK member whose idea was to micromanage everything "Just in case" and not wanting to bother anyone in her team as the pandemic "had changed them" and they were on furlough, so "why should I ask anything of them?". Bearing in mind that the cash flow could permit one of the team to work and support her, it was difficult for her to see how to start working differently. This is where coaching on a 1-to-1 basis works the best, as the systems and structure are the only ways this allowed her to step away from the business altogether and manage her business the way she dreamt of. I have done this time and time again with various micromanagers, and it works. It's all in the details of the operation and clear focus to achieve what we set out to do.

My aim is that by the end of the book, you will be able to apply those tools to your situation, whatever it may be. I believe that coaching is never one size fits all, as all business owners have their own ways of working, their own dreams to achieve and goals to strive for, but most of all have their own minds on how they process everything. With this book, I am hoping to reach and support as many micromanagers as possible, but of course, do get in touch if you need that extra one-to-one support.

Right now, I invite you to take a pen and paper, make your notes, review your situation throughout this book, and let me guide you to move forward in your way of thinking, plant some seeds to start acting differently, and allow you to revisit the way you function. The aim of this book is to become the leader you have always thought you could be. Since my background is in the spa & beauty industry, a lot of my examples are following such businesses. However, having dealt with many other entrepreneurs in many other industries, anyone can use these tips and techniques as long as they want to change their ways.

Imagine yourself doing what you were set out to do from when you started your business rather than being stuck in every detail of it all. Imagine yourself in that situation where you don't have to work all the hours you think you ought to in order to enjoy the fruit of your labor. Imagine yourself becoming the leader you want to be. Imagine that life could simply be a lot more well-balanced.

Valerie Delforge

International Business Strategy Consultant | The Delforge Group©

www.thedelforgegroup.co.uk

PART I

DEFINING MICROMANAGEMENT

1
WHAT IS MICROMANAGEMENT?

The Definition of Micro-Management

Before we start, I would like to assess what is happening at the moment. Since the pandemic, it is clear that the gap between employers and employees has deepened. What you cannot control makes you anxious, and since the pandemic was so intense for all of us, it highlighted unfairness and situations that we never had to deal with to this extent. The pandemic made us have to think of ethical business decisions that were new and somewhat intense, but most of all, it made us extremely reactive. Every night, worrying about what is going to happen, as an owner, you had the heavy burden to keep the business going. As an employee, it was a different story, but like I said to my clients, it was far from being a holiday. Some of your employees are worried, and mental health has never risen so much, so we must adapt to the situation, which is a true sign of leadership. I always look at my daughters in their 20s now and think, what must they experience at that age? What do they see? It's no wonder that they want a different way of life.

Now, coming out of a difficult period and entering an even more unstable and vulnerable one, even if you know that you must adapt, the lack of staff and change in the mindset of the employee has made business owners very cautious. From that comes control, which is a very fine line to become a micro-manager. Dealing with so many clients on an international level, I have seen a rise in micromanagement across the globe that reassures and contains situations, even if most owners I encounter want to work differently, and they too want to enjoy life.

You now have an opportunity to create the business you truly want. Maybe downsizing, maybe looking at a different way to reward your team and empower them to be more profitable, maybe reviewing the costs or offerings through a thorough analysis of your business (which is why I love 1-to-1 coaching so much as we can guide our clients through those changes). But the only way to do so is by becoming the proactive owner that will be able to enjoy a work-life balance and actually have a budget that works for your lifestyle. It is why I talk about the fact that leadership is at the core of everything you do and all of the soft skills you must develop to allow you to oversee the business rather than be part of the day-to-day operation and dealing with things you have grown out of. The key to all of this is to understand your style of management to generate trust in your business and create processes that will allow you to build what you want.

It's important to know that any business has an operational aspect. The more defined and detailed it is, the more it will allow your customer journey to be smooth and ultimately generate loyalty. My sole question to my members is: "How is it affecting the customer journey?"

I remember when I was the Head of Spa Operations for a large corporation, and one of my friend's daughters asked bluntly: "What does operation mean anyway?"

Ok, yes, so how can I define the operation to anyone, let alone a young mind, what it does and why is it so important? I guess for me, it is ultra-clear. For anyone who holds this job title, they would automatically know that all owners are dealing with operations but are not even aware of it.

I thought about it for a moment and replied:

 So I currently have eight Spas to look after but let's take the example of the biggest one with 50 staff members. Every day, we need to deliver the most incredible experience for our clients. They must feel that by the minute they secure their appointments to them coming to the spa as well as leaving after an amazing treatment, they have had the experience to remember forever and want to come back for more. We want them to leave feeling relaxed and refreshed as if they had a pause button from their lives and forgot about everything at that moment. It's a bit like Disney, we need to ensure that all they see is the magic but what it takes to make it happen, is down to the teams and how the operation is run.

The Spa consists of different teams that make that experience magical. Of course, it's about the therapists/aestheticians that deliver a wonderful treatment (at least we hope they do and we can measure that through various tools), but it's also about everyone working together to ensure that everything runs smoothly. For example, in

What is Micromanagement?

this particular Spa I was looking after, out of 50 staff members, only 26 of them were delivering treatments, the rest would help them deliver a customer journey that is detailed from the minute the client arrives at the spa to the minute they leave. If we really want to detail the customer journey, we can even say that it's from the minute they take conscience of the Spa and secure their bookings: Can they book online? Is that easy? Can they find the phone number? What's the phone call like? Are we confirming the booking? How? etc. to the minute they are at home: are we enticing them back to the Spa? What's the marketing strategy look like? How do we ensure that when they do come back, the customer journey and feel are consistent? How can we remain the best and entice them to stay with us?"

Her eyes glazed over, I realised that I needed to simplify my explanations and came back with this analogy:

> Imagine a beautiful three-tier cake. Well, a spa or salon team is just like that. But, as

mentioned, any business, especially those servicing clients, have this format...

The base of the cake is the owners/managers. They are the ones setting strong foundations for the operation/cake, creating procedures and processes, focusing on the budget from the money coming in to the money spent, managing different characters in the team to achieve a vision they have set, and ensuring everything is looked after, from towel management to cleaning of the spa/salon, stock control to managing the actual suppliers. The owner and manager have huge responsibilities as the buck stops with them. They are responsible for everything that is done or not done, and must create a strong ethos and culture so the way they want things to be run is implemented consistently, as consistency is the key to any repeat business. Achieving a vision can be done alone with outsourcing help if necessary, or with a team around you, but you have to ensure the team follows you. For that, your leadership skills are what will make a difference between a well-running spa/salon and an average, if not an awful one. Without a strong management team, the foundations are weak and the cake is in danger of crumbling at any point, which can result in terrible reviews from clients to unsatisfied staff. Management can be taught through processes, and leadership is a skill that you can learn, but these skills will have an impact on the business depending on how they are applied and ultimately received. You need to remember that even if you work alone, you still need to lead your business forward, and for that, the same principles apply: vision, processes, outsourcing, and the ability to overcome challenges.

Then comes reception, which is the middle of the tiered cake. Everything happens at reception; it's where the customer journey starts and finishes. Everything should go right at reception level, but you would be surprised how difficult it can be. It's where you make or break the money, as far as I am concerned. A good receptionist is worth their weight in gold. If you work alone, what happens at reception is still extremely crucial. No one likes me saying that, but I believe reception is possibly the hardest role to have, which is why we focus on it so much at The Delforge Group®. I should know; I did it for a long time when we first opened a brand-new salon in Zone 6 of London and didn't have the budget to hire a receptionist. My assistant and I valued that role so much that when we were able to hire the team once the cash flow was built, I can tell you that they became the most valuable members of the team.

As a receptionist, you take all the crap and none of the glory, basically. You have to deal with clients' demands, complaints, bookings, clients or staff members being late, demands from all angles, sickness, fed up, hyper, and even little divas with huge egos and so on. You have to deal with merchandising, cleaning, rota management, diary management, stock control, suppliers, deliveries, reaching your KPIs (Key Performance Indicators), managers, teams, and given set targets. No one comes and says to you, "Well done for such an amazing day, we not only achieved the targets with efficient diary management, but everyone is happy from staff to clients."

What is Micromanagement?

On the other hand, if you made a mistake with a booking, took too long to check someone in for some reason or another, had to deal with client complaints which made you run over your lunch hour and overlooked someone else's client, well, let me tell you that you will hear about it! You have to be a multi-tasker par excellence and remain calm under pressure, like a swan: calm, beautiful smile, and graceful, but underneath the feet are paddling through whatever is thrown at them at that moment. You have to learn how to avoid taking things personally and never crumble under pressure. You have to "Keep calm and carry on," as we say in the UK. This quote has never been so true for this role.

I believe that a good operation relies on these two teams: managers and reception. If the communication between the two is clear and defined, the organization is set so well that every detail is focused on, and you have a well-running Spa/Salon or any customer-facing business for that matter. As a consultant, when I get involved in a business, I look at these two teams before even looking at anything else. Are the processes in place so everyone knows what is expected of them? Are the receptionists supported by the managers, and vice versa? Are the communication and the tools used to communicate a hindrance or facilitate the smooth running of the operation? In all, if these two teams function well, you will find that the customer journey is spot on. If you have a business that doesn't require a reception team, the questions remain the same. Remember that it's all about the customer journey. What is the first impression you are giving that customer? Can you be satisfied with the customer journey as it stands?

Then comes the Therapists/Aestheticians/Nail technicians/Makeup Artists/Hairdressers, and basically anyone who delivers a service in exchange for taking money. They are the most important team, of course, as without them, we are unable to make the budget happen. The client comes here for a result whether they want to relax, look younger, feel better, or get ready to party, and they are the team with their magical skills. Every single one of them has a reason as to why they work in the business: for some, it is to earn money, some are career-driven, some simply want to get out of home in between the children's schooling hours, some have been in the industry for a long time, some are completely new, and some don't know why they are doing it; it seemed like a good idea at the time. And don't get me started on how the industry is viewed by many; that's another topic of conversation altogether!

The managers are the ones leading all of these characters towards a set vision and ethos, and that is where leadership skills matter so much.

Finally, we come to the cherry on top, the ultimate 5-star experience for the client. It's the feeling that a customer gets when they leave the premises, knowing that the service was exceptional, the results were amazing, and the team delivered beyond expectations. This is the difference between a job well done and a job that creates a lasting memory. Everything should be geared towards creating that magical feeling, so that the customer keeps coming back. We want to secure their loyalty over and over again, as customer loyalty is crucial to the success of a business, and the structure must be able to adapt to meet demand. The operational aspect of the business should be reviewed every year to ensure that everything is being delivered according to the standards you have set for the business.

I remember giving zero holidays to my managers in January so that we could focus on the strategies for the year ahead and ensure that the standards were met in all aspects of the operation.

The operation is the cream that binds everything together, the icing that unifies every team through systems and communication, and allows the customer to feel that everything is taken care of. The smoother the cream, the smoother the operation. In a spa/salon, the cream can be as simple as keeping everything clean: what are the teams responsible for, what is the cleaner (if you have one) responsible for, and what are the managers doing to ensure that this is delivered every time, all of the time? Every single day, regardless of staff sickness or other issues, it must be done. As a spa/salon, you must ensure that the client's experience is consistent. If I am a regular customer, I expect the same journey every time. If the spa/salon standards have dropped, I am quick to look elsewhere since I have more choices than ever as a consumer.

It is as simple as delivering the treatment on time for the customer to feel looked after. If it cannot be done, what procedures are in place to ensure that communication with the client is clear and timely? Stock management is the second most expensive element of the business after staff. If stock is managed sporadically, you will feel it in the budget and overspend. It is as simple as deciding on suppliers so that costs are kept within budget, but standards are never compromised.

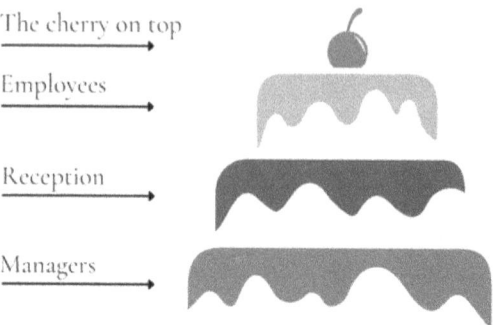

Left satisfied with this analogy, my friend's daughter made me realize that not everyone understands operations. A good operations manager can positively impact the customer journey and create a cherry on top without the client even realizing it. On the other hand, a disjointed operation due to terrible communication between teams and a lack of self-reflection will only plateau in growth and be taken over by fresh competition.

That's why I love one-to-one coaching - the personal approach to understanding the operation is essential to focus on areas of the business that will make a difference and increase profitability. The more money in the cash flow, the more flexibility there is to grow or even have a work-life balance for the owner. Every business is unique, and what makes it stand out is the owner, the concept, and how the operation is run.

Details such as when to offer water to clients, when to implement consultation, and team structure all play a critical role in delivering a strong operation.

The Delforge Group© has set everything around "The Delforge 5" - Budget, Leadership, Reception, Marketing strategy, and Retail culture. Operational decisions based on processes and procedures are critical to a manager's foundation, and even someone who is usually relaxed will eventually encounter operational issues that need resolving.

For example, before becoming a consultant, I was employed as a General Manager in a Spa that was in decline for over five years, but the concept was fascinating: a 1.5 hour appointment with an aesthetician who would do everything to make the client's skin look beautiful. After a consultation for the same amount of time, the treatment consisted of add-ons, such as microdermabrasion or an eyebrow shape, that the customer was informed about during the marketing and consultation. This spa was located in an affluent area of London and had a turnover of £2.2 million, with 35% retail sales. When I was employed as the Head of Spa Operation before I became a consultant, retail sales increased to 45%, making it a money machine. Sometimes, a team can be its own worst enemy, and with the pandemic, managing teams has become more challenging. However, managing teams is crucial to the success of an operation.

The culture of the team was such that the team members who generated the most revenue had the most influence and control. The director at the time allowed this culture to exist, which prevented any operational changes from being implemented as the team would push back against them.

Throughout this book, I will talk a lot about examples of this spa. Since I have had a lot of experience managing large teams as an area manager and regional manager prior to it, I can safely say that it is where all of my leadership skills were tested and came together to bring them to success. Within a year, we smashed last year's figures and overcame the target set by my director by a 6% increase on the set target. It was something that was unheard of for five years. Now, bearing in mind there was no money to invest, as with the decline came really poor cash flow, lack of new clients, and disjointed customer journey; I led the way forward for this disconnected team purely through defined operational aspects of the business as well as the strong vision I had set that was represented through very clear communication. My mindset had to be focused for the managers to become my ally to rally the troops and achieve what I had in mind for this brilliant but forgotten venture. For six months, I set and structured everything so the operation was to the high standards I wanted, reducing costs, and focusing on individual development, including key recruitment to bring in new fresh energy. I ensured that I felt comfortable with every detail of the operation and once everyone was where I wanted them to be, I was satisfied that I could bring in more clients. Of course, there will always be hiccups, times when everything happens all at once but if the foundations are strong and the systems are in place, there is something to fall back on. I could then go and network, build the trust back into the business from the chosen target market, and look at every opportunity that I could identify.

On my first day in the spa, having experienced the amazing facial which would have cost me £500 had I paid for it (never knew I needed so much work on my skin but my god it looked incredible and instantly had the brand running through my veins, I fell in love with the concept that my passion was literally ignited on day 1!!); I was told, "You are the ninth manager in 9 years… good luck!"

Okayyyyy… I thought, Set the tone, why don't you! Well done, Valerie, you always seem to find the job and team to give you a challenge!

I had carte blanche from my director as he didn't really know what to do with this Spa. It was so different from what he had dealt with before. So, after this facial, all I did was observe. For three weeks, I worked in every single team. I cannot provide services as I am pure management, but reception was a great place to start. I just looked at how everything functioned so I could understand how we were actually making money or losing it. As an owner, you know that decreasing the outgoings and increasing the revenue will be creating profitability, and managing cash flow will allow you to overcome situations. But what details of the operation allow us to do just that? To me, it's simple: analyzing the customer journey in detail will allow you to understand if the operation is answering everything we are delivering.

To manage a business to success is assessing and ensuring that everything we change within the operation is affecting the customer journey in a good way. This became one of my many sentences to my managers: "Okay, you want to do this, how is it going to affect the customer journey?"

I was told straight away, "Valerie, we need new towels, £20,000 worth, for that matter. They are old, falling into pieces, some have oil stains as old as the spa, and even if you wash them, they look awful."

Well, good luck finding £20,000 within a budget of a Spa that is in decline on top of everything! I thought.

I decided that the only way to find out was to work with the Spa attendants (the ones that help with cleaning and support the team, ultra crucial to the operation as they are the ones keeping the high standards). They were mortified, "Valerie, you shouldn't work with us, you are the GM!"

Think of that programme where the owner is going back to the shop floor. It allowed me on an entry-level to understand the challenges they were facing.

I noticed that dealing with the laundry, which had over 70 clients to serve, was a challenge on many fronts. Before the pandemic, disposable towels were starting to become popular, but even then, regular towels were still needed. The challenge was washing and drying these towels, which could easily add up and impact the budget. It's an operational dilemma that requires careful calculations.

It's important to avoid comparing your business to others, as each space has its own unique customer journeys, budgets, and dreams. During my observation, I found out that the dirty laundry was left in baskets in the staff room and then put in huge bags by the attendants, which were stored in a back corridor. This was not ideal, as the corridor was part of a fire exit and could cause problems during an inspection.

As I worked with the Spa attendant team, I discovered that the building manager was frustrated with us for blocking the corridor, but no one had communicated this to us. I believe that health and safety are often neglected because they are tedious and can be pushed to the end of the to-do list. However, hygiene standards are essential to the business and staff, and they must be given proper attention.

Regarding the towels, I realized that they were a daily nightmare for the attendants and the team. By 5 pm, we were using towels that were not so nice. I also found out that the laundry man was picking up the dirty towels at 6pm and bringing fresh ones at that time too. So, I called his manager and negotiated an additional £100 per week to come and pick up the dirty towels twice a day and bring fresh ones as well. This allowed us to have fresher towels, reduce the use of the back corridor, and spend a fraction of the £20k budget.

Of course, we still spent money on the towels that were literally hanging by a thread, but it was a manageable sum for the cash flow.

As you can see, a strong operation allows you to analyse and review all of the small details and ease the budget for cash flow and profitability purposes.

I have seen some shock horrors when it comes to operation and wanted to share these examples with you:

→ An evening event with 300 people invited and the glasses were not ordered resulting in panic and frantic search of glasses one hour before the event.

→ A cleaning company that were unable to cope with their staff sickness so the owner had to come in everyday to clean.

→ A supplier list that had never been revisited so the prices kept going up until I asked to shop around or renegotiate prices.

→ A reception team that was constantly bothered by the team to the stage where they were leaving after three months so recruitment and training was constant.

→ A client of mine working alone and finishing super late every evening until we got her a virtual PA to support her.

→ A team sent to a show to do hair and make up only for it to be starting two hours later and ultimately putting pressure on the team in the salon and clients waiting for them to come back.

→ I once had a staff member tell me that the stock comes in when she is in treatment so never knows what she should try and sell to the client.

→ A staff member had an accident and was off for two month and since everything was in her head no one had been trained for the specific work that she did.

Even more common ones:

→ The manager and reception team start at the same time as the team so the owner is the only one dealing with staff sickness at 7am in the morning and feels completely alone.

→ The receptionist team is doing their own opening and closing procedure so the team have no idea and are not told otherwise so most of the work is done twice.

→ The answering machine is not being checked and no customers are able to leave a voicemail as it is full.

→ Last month's offer on the A board outside is still there as no one knows what to write or takes ownership of it.

→ The team that feels hard done by because they have to clean everything after work.

It all relies on operational decisions that will make a difference to both the team and customers. To me, any business has an operational element that requires attention, which is why our business coaching applies to a wide range of industries, including spas, beauty salons, coffee shops, delicatessens, electricians, accountants, and more. As long as you're servicing clients, you have an operation to look after, including a staff and customer journey to decide on. The leader must focus on every single detail to create a smooth operation and engage their teams to deliver what is needed. The operational aspect of the business will allow you to create a structure so that as an owner, you can focus on building the growth of the business rather than being bogged down by the day-to-day tasks. It can get boring, tedious, and soul-destroying. I usually deal with burnt-out leaders who are so focused on the day-to-day that they have no idea why they started their business in the first place or how to grow it for the long term without being a part of it.

I have seen it again and again where leadership is trying to flourish, but the dream is quickly smashed by silly little things that make us feel awful or not aligned with the business anymore. Adding the pressure of social media to the mix, where everyone else seems to get it right, can make leaders feel deflated before the day even starts, dealing with issues as they occur or waiting for them to appear. I spoke to someone not long ago who dreads her phone pinging, especially in the morning, because she feels she will be finding out who is sick today. As the owner of four businesses, why is she the one receiving those messages? That's where the structure of the business and set operational procedures are crucial to protect both her mindset and dream. How on earth can her leadership grow if she is the one dealing with all of this?

I dealt with someone who contacted me because they heard me doing some public speaking at an event and felt so motivated that they went back to their vision that evening. But by the morning, they had to deal with clients being rude because the staff member was late, the delivery for stock not being delivered on time which generated some treatment changes, and cleaners who never came to clean. That vision seems like such a distant memory within one night.

―――

Running a business goes beyond the concept of simply selling a product through beautiful branding and marketing. To illustrate this, I'll give an example of an amazing Instagram account belonging to a clothes shop in France that one of my colleagues fell in love with. She followed their every move on social media and decided to visit the store while we were delivering training in that town. However, when she arrived, the customer service was so awful that the receptionist was on her phone, possibly worrying more about what was going to be posted on Instagram that day. The sizes were not all available, and the branding was nowhere near reflecting what was offered on Instagram. It was clear that my friend unfollowed the store straight away, never purchased anything, and will never go there again.

A good operational manager must deal with every aspect of the business, literally everything they have a say in. Since operations are the cream that sticks everything together, it is crucial that they understand how everything will be perceived, implemented, and even realistic within the business.

I believe that for leadership to happen, you must have the operational aspect of your business right, and from that, the structure that will allow your leadership to grow and flourish. Since the operational aspect of your role as an owner is to deal with everything, you must ensure that it doesn't all fall back onto you.

"A system isn't a system if it relies on one person" is one of my quotes that I keep reiterating to every client I speak to. In other words, everyone is dispensable but crucial to the operation. A good leader can walk away, go on holiday and the business still runs smoothly, the team still understands their expectations, and everyone is still focused on what needs to be achieved in order to build that dream they all bought into.

Now, let's add the pandemic to the mix. Here we have it: The rise of the micro-managers which has always been there to some extent but has been growing since there is a large gap that has formed between owners and staff during the lockdowns. Micro-Management has always existed but has never been so real and if we continue in that mindset, we will never empower the new generation to lead the way. Most of all, we will be our own block, our own worst enemy and will plateau rather than grow the business. We will constantly live in the "It was better before syndrome" that I have seen flourishing over the recent years. To me, every generation has given a challenge to the previous generation and there is nothing new there. I just spoke to my dad and his dad, and there were many issues in the 1960s they dealt with. Bridging the generational gap was hard to do.

What is Micromanagement?

Leadership has been spoken about for many years by incredible leaders that have found a way to build their dream and teams, and be flexible enough in their ways of thinking to overcome all challenges. But this gap that I am talking about has been extremely challenging in recent years. Everyone's perception of work has changed. I kept saying to my members: your team is experimenting with something other than a holiday; some are relaxing in the sun but some are really struggling. Mental health is real and I dread to think what it's like for the new generation that has only seen this. I look at my daughters and realize that their lives will be so different from mine. Now in their 20s, what do they see? Who can blame them if they want to put wellness before work? Who is right or wrong? As a leader, we simply must become flexible and adapt to the circumstances, which is a soft skill we will revisit at some point in this book.

The fact is that a lot of the time, we underestimate how operational the business is. To offer such smooth operation takes details, structure, and control. In any other industry that I am involved with, I can see it also resonates.

"The devil is in the detail," was how one of my bosses started his meetings. This stayed with me for a long time; actually, I still apply this in everything I do. No matter the industry, you must stand out from the crowd, feel that you have strong foundations to build on, and constantly satisfy your clientele. I saw a bakery in France open at 6am and close at 9pm with fantastic products. I was told it's a country where no one wants to work these hours, yet the owner manages it, and everyone smiles when you come to buy bread. What makes him so different? It can only be down to his leadership skills and clear operation.

Owners can become victims of their own success because everything is reliant on them. When it comes to the rise of micromanagers who are simply thinking, "I'd rather do it myself," "what is the point of training, they're gonna leave," "it's costing me money to train," "it's easier that way," "they don't understand," and so on, it is difficult for them to entertain a new way of working, even if they dream of it. Perhaps you have or are saying it now, but ultimately, the more you think that way, the more you are inviting that type of ethos.

As you will see throughout this book, micromanagers are complex and, in my opinion, unable to create long-term growth. They are hardly aware that they are behaving that way. They can be easily frustrated, but most of all, micromanagers want to manage every single aspect of the operation as no one can do it better. The pandemic only emphasizes that even more, especially with the recruitment issues. Add to that the feeling that no one wants to work anymore and wants to enjoy a work-life balance; it simply reinforces what the micromanager feels and thinks.

To me, micromanagement has many variants as to why we micromanage. I, too, was a micromanager at some point because I felt like everything was crumbling around me. I felt the need to control what I could control, what I knew by heart. When life is difficult around us, work tends to focus on the only thing that we know and are good at, especially if we are the owner of a business and built it all by ourselves.

As far as I can remember, I have always been keen to look at a challenge and analyze it from a 360° approach, which I learned by managing so many people. It's time to become flexible and adapt to a workforce that is telling you they want to change. Create an operation that responds to a different demand from your consumers. And most of all, I want this book to have a main message which is to take the time to reflect on the business like never before.

It's time to become the leader you wish you were, to lead the life you truly want and build the operation with strong foundations. After all, isn't that why you started your business in the first place?

So why focus on micromanagement, you may ask? How is it affecting the operation? Why is it becoming such an issue?

As mentioned, I believe that micromanagement is on the rise, and it will affect your staff and customer journey, but most of all, your work-life balance and mindset. It is the opposite of leadership as far as I am concerned. How can we empower the new generation to lead their lives? How can we empower ourselves to grow the business for the better so we can sustain cash flow and be proactive rather than reactive?

The more I deal with businesses, the more I realize that once the operation is set, it's down to the leader to keep empowering everyone around them. Most of the time, we are patching things hoping they will last for a while, putting out another fire that started whilst patching the last one… and the wheel carries on… So, it's so much better if I do it myself as I know what to do, and it's so much quicker. The fingers crossed management technique becomes more and more apparent. Can we really empower others if we micromanage to that effect?

What is Micromanagement?

Like a hamster on that wheel, there is a strong feeling of "no way out." Mixed with that the information overload, the rise of the coaches all shiny and sparkly that make you feel inadequate, the constant social media that tells you how everyone else has got it under control... Basically, it's easy for a micromanager to be born out of frustration and guilt. Analyzing the customer journey becomes the exercise that is only going to add to their to-do list, but guess what? I'd rather do it myself...

Let's examine what micromanagement entails and assess your current management style...

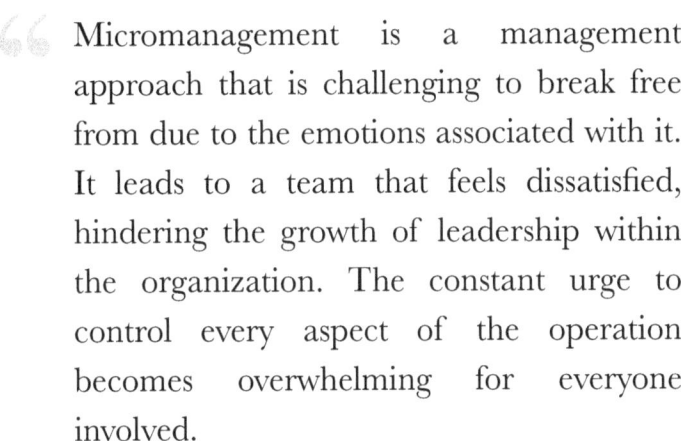

> Micromanagement is a management approach that is challenging to break free from due to the emotions associated with it. It leads to a team that feels dissatisfied, hindering the growth of leadership within the organization. The constant urge to control every aspect of the operation becomes overwhelming for everyone involved.

A micromanager understands this, but they are stuck in their old ways. Somewhere along the line, they know they need to change but are unsure of how to do so. It doesn't matter how many solutions are presented to them, it must be done their way. It's easy to see how we turn inward, especially in times of crisis. Most micromanagers I meet know they are micromanaging, but they can't help it. It's a feeling that is stronger than them, and they are simply unable to see how they can work differently.

Sometimes, a micromanager has someone helping them, but they are afraid of the fall. What if they leave? What if they do it wrong? What if they take all my ideas and run with them? The "what if" scenario takes over, and they revert to their old ways, micromanaging every single detail and overcompensating for everything the helper is trying to do. Trust is a massive issue, which we will revisit throughout this book.

In all, I believe that micromanagement is a rather complex style of management because one of its main aspects is a sense of needing to control everything. To me, it's simple: micromanagement is the opposite of leadership. It hinders the creation of leaders and stifles growth, and it only breeds frustration for everyone involved.

Here are the habits that I have noticed in the micromanagement style. You might relate some or all of them:

→ OVERCOMPLICATED SYSTEMS AND CREATING A PATTERN THAT ONLY SUITS THEM.

When it comes to operations, it's so important to focus on ease of systems so the customer or staff feels that everything runs fast and efficiently.

A micromanager tends to want to detail everything and even adds steps that are unnecessary to the process. I remember working for a company that had so many reports to create we ended up duplicating the information in four different forms. When I asked why this was necessary, there were no clear answers. I believe that different departments wanted different reporting with the same information, but ultimately, this added at least three hours to my Monday admin day. Was this Micromanagement? Yes, because when looking for a solution to what seems like a pointless exercise, my manager was in a micromanagement style of "never question the system". The inflexibility of processes and over-complicated systems means that not only time management is overlooked but the system itself is stopping growth. You had to be square, god forbid if you had a round idea that would actually work. This becomes an over-complicated system or one that is purely reliant on the micromanager, which makes them feel so much better and a sense of importance within the operation. I have met some micromanagers, especially within a corporate environment, that were ensuring that the system in place was reliant on them to give them a sense of worth and show the boss that nothing can be done without them. I see it in smaller businesses where there is little sense in the system, but it gives a sense of control if nothing else, and it tends to overshadow anyone else's skills. We all know that a leader creates leaders, but a micromanager ensures that everyone does what they are meant to do and nothing else.

→ SYSTEMS THAT RELY PURELY ON THEM AND NO CHANGES ARE ALLOWED.

This is true of most micromanagers who are finding that their system is the best as well as being completely closed to a new system that might actually improve the staff or customer journey. I give you a simple example: when discussing with one of my members that the manager should be responsible for the first step of recruitment, she said that they wouldn't know what to look for. When I asked her whether it could be a good idea to give the managers a set of requirements and create a strong procedure for recruitment with key questions to ask, she was absolutely horrified. Surely the manager would be inefficient at knowing how to recruit and anyhow, the manager will never have time to do the first interview. I already know that too many changes with my micromanagers sometimes are counter-productive so I tend to change the way things are done one step at a time. So I said ok, let's at least ensure that the manager is the one dealing with the trade test (test to check how amazing the skills of the candidate are) and deal with the trial so you can either come at the end of the trial if the manager feels the candidate is worth it and wants to put her/him/they forward. Palpitations, cold sweats, it's impossible to ask for someone else to do that, even if they are managers, that's just too much. Valerie, I must ensure we get the right person in. During our conversation, I asked her if she had ever hired the "wrong person," and she admitted that she had. When I inquired about how she handled that situation, she confirmed that she had indeed managed it, but it was challenging for her mindset to accept that she had made such a mistake. Micromanagers typically find it unthinkable to make mistakes, and the idea of hiring the "wrong person" for a job can be highly destructive for them. She also argued that at least she will only have herself to blame. In all, an argument that made sense in her head but was quickly destroyed by my thought process: are you looking to step out of the business three days a week? Yes. So then you need to trust the process you are putting in place. Now? She only deals with the last interview process and trusts the system.

→ POOR TIME MANAGEMENT AND LACK OF EFFICIENCY.

Since micromanagers focus on every detail and insist on being involved in everything, time management can suffer dramatically. I've seen many examples of this, but one that stands out is a client who spent two hours every week shopping for groceries for her spa, convinced that everything had to be done by her. When I suggested that she order groceries online and delegate the task to one of her receptionists, it took her two months to accept the idea. Once she saw how effective it was, however, she never looked back.

Overly complex systems and micromanagement can work against us by creating unnecessary work and preventing growth. To avoid these problems, it's important to regularly analyze our operations and strategies, and make adjustments as needed to improve efficiency and streamline processes.

. . .

What is Micromanagement?

→ NO WORK-LIFE BALANCE AND NO SWITCHING OFF.

Well, this goes hand in hand with poor time management, but it is also deeper than that. I believe that work can become an addiction, and for our micromanagers, it can certainly be very tricky to offload from the day-to-day operation. The work-life balance suffers since nothing can run smoothly and efficiently without the micromanager involved. I had a client who went to her business every single Saturday before closing time to check that everything went smoothly, even though it was meant to be her day off with her children. When I asked her why she felt the need to do that, she couldn't provide any valid answers and even realized that what she was saying made little sense. Since the operation is unable to function properly without the micromanager, the constant worry is the most concerning. Not being able to switch off takes its toll after a while and also becomes a habit.

→ NO ROOM FOR ERRORS AND GROWTH THAT HAS REACHED A CERTAIN PLATEAU.

The classic micromanagement style is one where there is no point in asking for help, as the micromanager believes that others will make mistakes anyway. I had another client who decided to create an event, and I encouraged her to delegate it to a senior staff member so we could see how they would lead the operation. However, halfway through, my client became frustrated with the lack of communication and what she perceived as slow progress, and took over the event herself, even contacting the suppliers herself and not giving the senior staff member a chance to do it. When I caught up with the senior staff member, she said to me, "I thought I was making good progress, but it seems that whatever I do is never good enough." This not only crushes the staff's self-esteem but also reinforces the micromanager's belief that if they don't do it themselves, it will never be done properly or on time.

→ IT'S LONELY AT THE TOP AND THEY CAN'T SEE CLEARLY WHERE THEY ARE GOING.

This is the consequence of micromanagement where there is a constant need to feel reassured that things were going their way. A client of mine had decided to employ a manager who was instructed to report to her every single morning and evening. An email was meant to be sent at the beginning and at the end of the day. Needless to say, the manager was so worried about

What is Micromanagement?

these emails, she was only focusing on them. She didn't last very long in that role.

When I challenged my client as to why she needed those emails daily, she simply said: "I just want to make sure I am spending my money on someone that thinks like me". Complete control and fear are far from empowering for the manager but most of all create a tension that is generating a sense of fear.

I find that most micromanagers want validation in their decision-making process that they are doing the right thing; however, poor decision-making is isolating them even more. The more they behave that way, the more they are unable to see where they are going in the long term. The vision is very blurry. Yes, I grant you that some micromanagers have a clear vision, but unfortunately, it ends up being a vision that is purely focused on them and far from being empowering for anyone around them. I am sure they can't even see people around them when they visualize their future!

Another example here happened to me! I had a three-month contract with a business where the owner would watch my every move on camera, then call me to check whether I was lying about where I was or what I was doing. The meetings I was having with each team member were completely frustrating her, taking too long as far as she was concerned, but I knew it was because she hadn't been involved in them, so she called me in between and during those meetings to ensure I would be discussing what she thought was the most important. Total control of what is being said and how management needs to repeat her words to the team means that she will always plateau in her growth. You do need to be open to change if you want to change. In this instance, change was never going to happen unless it is forced upon as burnout would.

→ MULTI-TASKING IS FAR FROM BEING A PRODUCTIVE AND THINKING THERE ARE NO OTHER WAYS.

"Multitasking is the art of messing up several things at once" is one of my favorite quotes that I read years ago, and I believe you can see that in micromanagement-style businesses. This client of mine was the queen of messaging, sending everything to her manager as she thought of it. The idea would be that "I am going to forget to tell her that, so I'll pop it on a message." This would be great only if it wouldn't overwhelm her manager. Frustration mounted up from my client when things weren't done on time or forgotten about, but the manager felt she was unable to do anything else she had to do until she had dealt with all the messages. Trying to multitask, the manager was ultra-stressed and felt that she needed to ensure the operation was looked after and was capable of doing that but also that communication with her boss was paramount, so she spent a lot of time pleasing everyone.

Another client example: she had written the weekly to-do list for the managers of her five salons and then got frustrated when they couldn't achieve it. When I looked into it, they only had one hour a week to achieve everything. The micromanager seems to be setting their teams up for failure and not trusting they can deal with their own time management. Therefore, multitasking becomes the forefront of everything, and the feeling that it's the only way to do things adds pressure on the managers and nothing else.

―――――

In all, what is interesting is that there is little psychological research done on the psychology of micromanagers themselves. This is despite around 80% of surveyed people reporting having worked for a micromanager, so where are they? We all know someone or know we have been or possibly are like this at the moment, but it's actually hard to find self-reports of a micromanager.

Culturally taboo, people will go to great lengths to avoid ignoring or even dismissing claims. Anonymous feedback from staff can often be the only way to find out, but of course, the manager can dismiss these also as the truth is sometimes very hard to hear, let alone having to change their ways. A micromanager will find that too hard to even think of, even if they are sometimes dreaming of the day when everything will run without them.

Feel free to write to us with some more examples. We are collecting them for further studies of this management style and proof that it will become a block in your growth.

The key for this book to have an impact on your behavior is to be honest with yourself so you can develop your leadership style, and part of that is to look into our weaknesses to make them strengths.

For now, let's score your micromanagement style! Just to see where you are at and what we will need to work on together…

What is Micromanagement?

Score your Micro-Management

Every tick you have, score yourself 1 point and add them up at the end.

I'd rather do it myself because...

- ❏ It's quicker if I do it myself
- ❏ I have no one to help me
- ❏ Unsure where to start
- ❏ No one knows the reports I need.
- ❏ I wake up and start working
- ❏ I work over the weekends
- ❏ I work in the evening after my day is finished
- ❏ I delegate but get frustrated so I take over
- ❏ It takes too long to train someone
- ❏ I create my manager's to do list
- ❏ I finish my to do list quickly
- ❏ I check the security cameras regularly
- ❏ I stalk other businesses and they are managing better than me
- ❏ I'll do it now quickly

I'D RATHER DO IT MYSELF

- ❏ I never fully trust someone

- ❏ I have never found out what skills my team have

- ❏ I have had too many bad experiences with managers

- ❏ I need constant updates when I delegate something

- ❏ I trust it will never be as good as what I can do

- ❏ Everything is in my head

- ❏ Individual meetings are useless

- ❏ Team meetings are about figures and information

- ❏ I do meetings but they are tedious

- ❏ I am scared to change my ways

- ❏ I have 0 idea what I should delegate

- ❏ I don't need help

- ❏ I have always functioned this way and it's worked so far

- ❏ I am fully prepared to change but I am scared

- ❏ I am afraid that I will lose it all

- ❏ I always work on holidays

Write your score here: ………

. . .

1 - 9

Well done! You are the micromanager that needs tweaking in their process and seems to be open to change...

Or are you?! Have you answered correctly? What if you gave this test to your team? Would they score you the same as you are scoring yourself?! You have picked up this book for something though, so maybe somewhere along the lines, you are aware that something might need tweaking... This book will help you to refine your management style and learn a few tools to generate an even smoother operation or even help the micromanager you know who is functioning this way.

10 - 19

On the brink of feeling overwhelmed, your management style is getting the better of you at times. You are fully aware that you need to grow differently, but possibly confused about where to start. This book will help you make headway in the change you are looking for. After that, it's about trusting that you are implementing the correct systems for your leadership to grow. Keep on learning about leadership to keep growing; never stop and revisit your structure to ensure it allows you to keep growing.

19 - 25

Ok, now you are dealing with everything, and it's starting to work against you. It's time for drastic change and to revisit how you are working. My advice is to write down for a whole two weeks what you are doing and revisit where you are wasting time and what can be delegated. Read the book first, put "Your ducks in a row," and then go for it. You can do this; you are reading the book for a reason, and that is because you know you want to change in order to grow. Persevere and analyze every year. Read the book again and again, especially the tools you are failing at, and don't stop opening yourself up to overcome your overwhelming sensations. Have you considered being coached?

26 - 30

The Micromanager! So you have identified yourself as the key Micromanager who is in urgent need of change, even on the brink of burnout if you are not careful. It's important to know that you are not alone in your journey, read the book as it's time to reassess your work mode. Creating a path to success will come through your operation and unless you reach out to a coach, family, friend, or support network, you might find the isolation stops your growth. Time for radical changes. Unless you are happy as you are, in which case you might simply not be ready for change, hopefully this book will start some of the process for constructive change.

Now, it's time to confess…

Find a notepad and write down in bullet points how you are functioning currently. As you go through this book, you will be able to highlight what to work on as priorities.

- ➔ Example 1: My time management suffers with the children at home and having to juggle my work-life balance.
- ➔ Example 2: I spend most of my weekends working to get on top of things.
- ➔ Example 3: I have two managers with titles because I didn't want to lose them but they don't help me.

Let's review this information later on in the book. Firstly, let's delve into understanding why we micromanage this next chapter…

2

WHY DO WE MICROMANAGE?

What is interesting is that a leader must develop greater strategic abilities to foster business growth. However, for our micromanagers out there, acquiring a new set of skills can be challenging. These skills are unique and often contradictory to operational skills and capabilities. Micromanagers frequently rely on the same skillsets that initially propelled them into their current positions, as it is easier to remain within the comfort zone of familiar operational territory. This preference for familiarity is often tied to established habits and a desire for control.

"What got you here won't get you there" is a clear mindset to adopt but micromanagers are unable to think differently.

One aspect of micromanagers is that they can act in a place of fear.

→ FEAR OF NEGATIVE OUTCOMES

Motivated by fear of failure and public embarrassment and being out of the loop. This fear is inflated by the fact they probably excelled originally which is what got them promoted/where the manager is today.

→ FEAR OF BEING UNINFORMED/DISCONNECTED

They fear of losing touch of the real stuff as they often believe operational are important to hold onto by overcompensating and asking for too many reports which helps reduce anxiety and by creating confusion among staff members as they don't understand the rationale behind reports or why managers are sitting in on meetings they never need to attend in the first place.

→ FEAR OF LOSS OF CONTROL

"Your title gets bigger but your personal control gets smaller". They will want to over compensate. The irony of power when you feel secure in your power you never feel compelled to control everyone around you. There is also a sense of urgency here; they like to control time and other people's use of time.

→ HEALTHY EGO THEORY

Bosses start careers as high performers. They were experts in their roles but now managing a group that will never be as good as them as it will make them look bad and make them put their name on something which average which in itself is out of the question.

So, there you have it, micromanagers are complex in their emotions and the emotions that impacts on others.

It's now time to introduce you to Marc and Marie, micromanagers par excellence who encapsulate the traits of Micromanagers. Marc and Marie are fictional characters, but their stories are true and will be used as examples throughout this book.

Marie is in her 40s and has owned a beauty salon for 15 years, which she set up with her wife, Tanya. They put the money down together to rent premises for the salon, which is located about 30 minutes away from their home. Tanya works in investment banking and provides Marie with maintenance and moral support, but Marie feels disconnected from her because she is unable to fully explain her day-to-day stress and constant worries. Marie feels like she never has enough time in the day, despite having three teenage children to look after and no financial worries. Tanya encourages Marie to turn off her phone and enjoy time with the family, but Marie resists because she feels like she can't.

Marie's salon has been successful for a long time, employing eight staff members, including two full-timers, four part-timers, a full-time receptionist, and a Saturday receptionist. However, Marie's main issue is the lack of structure within her team. Her staff is established and used to Marie's micromanagement style, but they don't fully support her. Marie has never created systems because everything relies on her input, and she prefers to keep everything in her head. The atmosphere in the salon can suffer, and Marie doesn't understand why her team is less motivated about their careers. As far as Marie is concerned, everyone performs, so she lets things flow. She works in treatments four days a week and has one day for admin, but clients expect her to be there all the time.

Why Do We Micromanage?

Marie constantly feels like things are better when she's there, even on her days off or during vacations.

Marie tried to employ a manager or get one of her senior staff to be more involved, but she ended up going back to her old ways because it was more comfortable for her. She never took the time to explain her expectations because she didn't have the time for anything else but her own work. Marie's children are growing and need more attention with their studies, but she is unable to change and constantly feels guilty about everything she has done or should have done. Marie feels comfort in controlling her business, and any change would be a risk because it could crumble around her. She updated her appointment system about four years ago and has shiny new reports to look at, but she doesn't know what to do with them. Marie micromanages her staff for every move, but their performance is never really monitored. It takes too much effort to introduce someone new to the team, so she would rather keep things as they are than go through the motions of recruitment.

Marc is in his mid-30s and has owned four hair salon businesses for over 12 years. He owns two of the buildings, while the other two are concessions in big department stores scattered across four towns. This can be difficult in terms of time management and dealing with the various aspects of different operations for each business.

When he started out, he was ambitious and his silent business partner was his girlfriend. They were happy to create a strong business model with the vision of opening one salon per year. However, after a messy separation five years ago and having to buy his girlfriend out of the business, Marc is now on his own dealing with the four salons. Although one could argue that each salon manager supports him, Marc still creates their to-do list every week, checks every single detail, and wants to know everything that's happening.

Since his separation, Marc has become more and more focused on his businesses. The hurt he went through has made him trust no one to take care of things, so all systems are down to him. He keeps everything in his head, as the salons never received any updates due to the payouts he had to do. At the moment, if it's not one salon, it's another that requires his attention. He seems to love the control as it gives him a sense of purpose, even though he's on the brink of burnout but unable to admit it.

His managers know that he needs to be involved in every single detail, even down to the changing of a lightbulb. Marc still requires all of his staff to communicate with him directly so he knows what's happening. He can't even answer the question of why he has managers. His vision has become extremely blurry, and even if he wants to open more salons, it seems like a distant future as he's lost direction.

Marc employs 32 staff across the salons, some employed and some self-employed. This can be quite challenging as he has little control over the latter. He's trying to recruit, but finds it very difficult to find personalities he can connect with. Since every salon has its own way of dealing with the day-to-day operations, the over-complicated paper-based system means that he's been unable to take time off without receiving a message from one of his staff.

Although he loves his business and it's the only thing that's kept him going all these years, the financial pressure and lack of clarity have made him one of the most extensive micromanagers.

The Trust Issue

A lot of Marc and Marie's out there have a huge trust issue.

Here are several signs that we can have trust issues:

- You assume betrayal. ...
- You await betrayal. ...
- You are overly protective. ...
- You distance yourself from others. ...
- You avoid commitment. ...
- You never forgive the smallest mistakes. ...
- You are excessively wary of people. ...
- You feel lonely or depressed...
- You have had a bad experience in the past
- You feel weak if you trust someone

Some of the Marc & Marie's I know have definitely had some of these feelings in their way of functioning. Knowing who to trust is one thing, but how to trust is another which can be very difficult for our Marc and Marie.

So, where does this trust issue come from? A number of elements play a part...

→ THE PAST

Maybe they have been burnt in the past and cannot get over that. This can really be crippling to Marc and Marie as they are finding it really difficult to trust again, regardless of who they might have in front of them. Every time I dealt with someone in this situation, I manage for them to open up to trust someone with the tools I will give you in this book.

→ NO ONE IS GOOD ENOUGH

They are simply unable to comprehend what another person can bring to the table, and they will never believe that someone else can do the jobs that are needed as well as they do. This is why they tend to find flaws in everyone they meet or even feel overwhelmed by the thought of working differently. Marc and Marie are only able to trust their way of working, not to trust someone else's way of doing things.

One day, Marie thought that one of her staff members could do some admin work for her as she was finding it difficult to cope with the workload. Reluctantly, she gave the tasks to the staff member, but she checked everything to the minute details afterwards. It took her twice as long, and she might as well have done it herself!

. . .

→ CONTROL

Being in control gives them a sense of accomplishment. Also, being in control of someone gives them power, and power gives a sense of capability. But why do we have such a strong need for control? I find this fascinating, as it is the root of micromanagement.

These are complex feelings, and unless you heal from them and are ready to change, they will constantly block your growth. But understanding how to put the systems in place given in this book, as well as dealing with your mental health, is crucial to explore these points above if you find that these feelings are taking over.

Let's bear in mind here that being in control of your business from a leader's point of view means being connected with your values and vision and setting meaningful goals for yourself. By being productive and delegating in an efficient manner, you become more engaging with everyone around you. You can tackle and solve problems more easily and ultimately achieve beyond your expectations.

In my experience, leaders who micromanage often have insecurities about their capabilities as a leader. Hence, why control gives them a sense of power.

Time Is Not On My Side

→ TIME MANAGEMENT

Marc and Marie have zero time for anything, let alone working on achieving a work-life balance. They are constantly inundated with work as they simply have too much to do. Some micro-managers may argue that they are fine and able to handle everything in a timely manner, but in my experience, restructuring the micromanagement approach can lead to amazing growth. By empowering these managers to delegate tasks and trust their employees, they can grow themselves and their businesses beyond what they thought possible.

Time management is complex, and I have found that it can be difficult to train someone with time management issues to break away from old habits. This is especially true for micromanagers, as they are often even more resistant to change. However, implementing effective time management strategies and delegating tasks can ultimately lead to increased productivity and success for both the manager and the business.

→ NO TIME TO TRAIN

Marc and Marie might struggle with training effectively because they can easily become frustrated. Moreover, since the systems rely heavily on them, training might seem like an extra burden on their already busy schedules. For instance, when Marc attempted to train his receptionist on some paperwork, he quickly grew impatient when the paperwork was returned with errors. Although he spent two hours training her, he never followed up or provided feedback. Instead, he communicated sporadically with her for six weeks before deciding that the effort was not worth it. As a result, Marc continued doing his own reports, reaffirming his belief that it was better to do things himself.

→ NO TIME FOR ERRORS

Well, let's make time management the main issue here. If Marc and Marie give a task away, there is no time to retrain, so errors are seen as a huge deal. In a way, when someone makes mistakes, it only reinforces their attitudes: "I told you it is better if I do it myself!" By never wanting to give up time to grow the team, they will lead them to stagnation.

Marc managed to make his receptionist feel bad and stressed about the whole reporting, but he also overlooked the need for engagement. Very soon, the receptionist became disgruntled and unhappy in her work, fearing every time Marc was asking her something, and she ended up leaving.

Building Blocks

→ MONEY

The biggest one of them all is money. Marc and Marie are so much in control of their finances that they cannot see the value in spending more money on having someone to help them. This becomes the perfect excuse to reinforce their attitudes towards management, and if they do decide to invest, there should be zero room for errors.

→ NOT ABLE TO LET THINGS GO

Like everything listed above, the main impact I feel from this is the lack of vision. Living in the past and trying to control everything in their path is a clear sign of being unable to grow for the future.

→ UNABLE TO RELAX

Thinking of one thing to do per minute creates a sense of an overwhelmed mind, with the need to constantly be on the go. Marie has suffered from burnout before but reverted to her old ways as she was unable to create a system to support her. The phrase "I just need to do this" is constantly in her vocabulary.

→ GUILT

It's really important to work on this as it is an emotion that is going to constantly work against Marc and Marie. They constantly feel guilty about not achieving enough, which is quite tiring. Guilt is usually associated with anxiety and the need for control.

→ FRUSTRATION

Everything breeds frustration as the expectations are never met. Again, the cause of anxiety and inability to see how they can grow.

. . .

➜ COMPARISON

Constantly comparing ourselves only adds pressure to the work we're trying to do. It's a huge issue nowadays and adds to everything we're already feeling. While I always feel that comparing yourself is useless, sometimes Marc & Marie are unable to help it as it's everywhere they look: social media, new businesses in town, and friends telling them about their experiences elsewhere. The growth of experts in their fields gives them a sense of complete inadequacy, which only multiplies their need for control. All in all, it's a recipe for disaster.

➜ THE EGO

The ego can be a difficult issue to address because not every Marc and Marie will suffer from an inflated ego, but somewhere along the line, the ego is getting in the way. When deployed properly, the ego can also help us grow, but in Marc and Marie's case, it's keeping them very busy in their own minds, and feeding the ego becomes the only way they can function.

Habits

➜ WORKING UNDER PRESSURE

Marc and Marie love working under pressure; it's how they have always functioned, and it's what they know. Somehow, they are able to deliver every time, and the more work they have, the more they can manage. But at what cost? Working under pressure can be obsessive, and it becomes the only way for them to function and get work done.

➜ CREATE A SYSTEMATIC APPROACH TO THEIR WORKLOAD

The sheer thought of delegation and working differently sends shivers down Marc and Marie's spines; it's simply inconceivable. Even if they feel overwhelmed and know deep down inside that they need to change their approach to their work, they are unable to work towards it. They have a systematic way of dealing with their to-do list, with various colors indicating things only they can understand. Some of them have one diary for appointments, one for the to-do list, one pad for the team, and another for training; it's everywhere, and only they know what to do and where to look. Marc and Marie like everything their way and their way alone, and the workload will be dealt with as they say.

→ UNABLE TO SEE THE WOODS FOR THE TREES

Despite thriving to work under pressure, Marc and Marie are bogged down with the day-to-day operations and whatever latest pressure they have put upon themselves. Their vision is blurred by the simple fact that they are too focused on their giant to-do list. Their sense of perfectionism is taking over, and they are prioritizing the smallest details as no one else can do better than them.

→ THE FEAR OF CHANGE

It takes 66 days to form a new habit, so it's difficult for Marc and Marie to keep going for that long if they are trying to change. Their micromanagement takes over, and they go back to their default system: control, control, control! When I meet a micromanager and see the signs, I know it's going to be a long road before we can change their habits. I have to say that the fear of change is one of the most relevant to Marc and Marie's management style and is usually linked to all of the above mentioned. The fear of the unknown can be crippling and create a feeling of anxiety that is difficult to overcome. It's what I would call a vicious circle. They may want to change, but the fear and anxiety make them go back to their safe place. The question is, are they ready for change?

Confession Time!

As a hairdresser, you can create a mood board for various events or even if you want to create your own photoshoot. A mood board consists of photos, textiles, colors, etc., intended to evoke or project a particular style or concept.

One day, Marc admitted that he had a mood board in his office that was 15 years old... When I looked into it, years and years of mood boards were stuck in the corner of the office. Not only did it take up a lot of space, but it was also old-fashioned, overwhelming, and unnecessary!

But for Marc, it was impossible to get rid of... "Just in case I need one of them."

Cluttered in the corner, Marc knew what I was going to say but was looking at me with fear and anxiety in his eyes. "Ok, I can see they are very important to you. Why don't you take photos of them and keep them in a digital folder? Keep the last two years so you have them at hand but get rid of the rest. Ok, I can see this is giving you palpitations, keep the last two years and put the rest in your loft or stockroom so at least the office stays clear of clutter."

Happy with this compromise, Marc realized that letting go and using technology was actually feeling quite good, and a clear office was really much better for her mindset when he entered the room.

Now, let's look at the consequences of micromanagement…

3
THE CONSEQUENCES OF MICROMANAGEMENT

The Work-Life Balance

The biggest issue of all is the lack of balance. It's like a vicious circle that is difficult to break out of. Unable to differentiate between work and life will leave Marc and Marie feeling completely overwhelmed, even if they can bring themselves to admit it. Working on your business can be addictive, which in itself feeds the need for micromanagement. That's where I found that most micromanagers will function from work to life in the same way. The problem with the work-life balance is the lack of clarity. No headspace, no step back to analyze where and what to do next, which gives a blurry purpose and vision.

The Flossy Syndrome

Let me introduce you to Flossy, a character that I created whilst doing a lot of public speaking and realised that I was giving real names and this could get me into trouble at some point!

The fact is, micromanagement is difficult for anyone to endure as this style of management, as described in the previous pages, is destroying more souls than empowering future leaders.

"Flossy could be difficult."

When I defined Flossy and her ways, I looked at the word difficult and all of the synonyms that came with it.

Synonyms[1]

troublesome · tiresome · trying · exasperating · demanding · unmanageable · intractable · perverse · contrary · recalcitrant · obstreperous · refractory · fractious · unaccommodating · unhelpful · uncooperative · unamenable · unreasonable · disobliging · stubborn · obstinate · bull-headed · pig-headed · hard to please · hard to satisfy · fussy · particular · over-particular · fastidious · perfectionist · critical · hypercritical · finicky · awkward · cussed ·

choosy · picky · bloody-minded · bolshie · stroppy · balky · contumacious · froward · contrarious · finical

I didn't understand Froward. I wondered if there had been a typo and it should be Forward but then thought that a Flossy is the opposite of Forward so I looked into it…

Froward · stubborn · headstrong · willful · unyielding · inflexible · unbending · intransigent

We all know someone, and I am sure that now you have someone in mind and can identify a face to those words. And if you think of micromanagement, it is a style of management that is very difficult to endure for the team, so the word "difficult" becomes true for our Marc and Marie.

Now, there are a few words I would like to look into deeper here, as they are really key to understanding that the Flossy syndrome can be complex, which therefore has a different level of impact.

→ PERVERSE

I find that interesting when we talk about someone being difficult. Are Marc and Marie perverse to the point that they want people they delegate to will be failing? It could be unconsciously happening but I believe this reassures them and validates that the way they work is the only way they should work. Power to their ways, forget new ways as they never work anyhow!

→ PERFECTIONIST

Now that's interesting. I'm pretty sure that in my days of managing people, I was a Flossy to my management team and quite demanding. If being a perfectionist makes someone difficult to work with, we can see why this is linked to micromanagement and how it can affect everyone. Are you a perfectionist? Is that affecting every task that you are trying to do as it's never good enough?

→ CRITICAL

This is certainly the most difficult aspect, as sometimes, Marc & Marie are critical without even realizing it. I believe that sometimes they will find issues when there are none, and even anticipate issues without trying to delegate or work differently. Until they let that go, they will constantly feel unsatisfied with their work. They are their own biggest critic, and that, in itself, can be very tiring for everyone involved.

→ TIRESOME

You must be conscious that this style of management is tiresome for all involved, and until you have acknowledged that, it will be difficult to make a change. When the work environment is exhausting to work in, staff turnover can be high, or the existing team may become accustomed to the way things are, unable to develop or progress, and will continue to accept this work culture. This will ultimately lead to issues in the long run, and I guarantee that staff performance will suffer at some point.

The Team

Being on the receiving end of micromanagement can suck the fun out of day-to-day work, as it creates a negative work culture. Marc and Marie may be skilled at manipulating those around them, allowing them to maintain control and have things done their way.

So how do they affect the team on a day to day basis?

➜ Lack of motivation to try anything new, resulting in no innovation

➜ Damages the employee's trust

➜ Creation of habits that are unhealthy

➜ Stress, frustration, burn outs

➜ Decrease in productivity

➜ Nit-picking every details

➜ Redoing the work already completed

➜ Scalability is unthinkable and non existent

➜ Resentment

➜ High turnover of staff

Ultimately, this means that the employee is less likely to speak positively about the business they work in and unlikely to recommend its products or services to their friends or as a good place to work. They will not see themselves as being part of the organization and will be less engaged in anything that is asked of them.

The worrying aspect of micromanagement is the culture that it breeds and the stifling of independent thinking. The lack of ownership becomes apparent and can be suffocating for anyone who tries to make changes happen. Marc and Marie contribute to this culture by stamping on individuality, it's in their nature and they simply can't help it.

It's Lonely At The Top

I believe that is the main aspect of micromanagement. However, it's very hard to define as, like anything, our Marc and Marie got used to being on their own, and in any case, they prefer it! Nonetheless, it's ultra-lonely at the top, and the lack of sharing, discussing, and leading is completely out. "My way or no way" ultimately brings staff members to eventually avoid them completely when it comes to support. Marc & Marie have been used to it, so they know no difference. Anything that will bring them unity with teams will probably be too scary, and therefore they constantly reassure themselves to behave a certain way. Marc & Marie have completely accepted the way they function and are in full agreement with their behavior to the detriment of everything else around them.

No Growth Allowed

One of the results of micromanagement is the lack of growth from all angles. Whether it is for themselves or their team, nothing will be able to grow as there will be far too many changes, which is not great for Marc and Marie. Their behavior will not only make them plateau but their business will also suffer. Growth becomes limited, if not impossible, and definitely rather difficult.

Confession Time!

"Marie was on her way to work one day, super early as she had an event to manage. She realized that no one was helping her but knew it was better this way so she could be in charge of it all, which she preferred anyway. Feeling rather nervous and super anxious about it all, she knew that by coming in early, she would make the most of her day. When the event happened, Marie ordered everyone to do what needed to be done. It was like a military operation that was defined by the minute. Was it fun? Was it team bonding? Was it exhausting? Was it fruitful? Marie simply said: "It was okay. I was busy worrying about everything else and never managed to meet all of the people I wanted to as I was busy with the small details."

Marie seems to have difficulty enjoying her job, and the lack of support only reinforces this feeling. She believes it's better if she *does everything herself anyway, and her perfectionist tendencies may prevent her from celebrating any positives from the event.*

---

1. Oxford Languages

PART II

THE SOLUTIONS TO MICROMANAGEMENT

4

LEADERSHIP IN AN OPERATIONAL BUSINESS

Six Leadership Styles

"Leadership is the art of getting someone else to do something you want done because he or she wants to do it." Dwight Eisenhower said this, and it's one of my favorite quotes. It's certainly true that when leading a team, you need to get them to work for and with you, and the key is to constantly empower them in some way or another.

Leadership is a word that gets thrown around a lot, but do we really know what it is? And do we know how to become the kind of leader people want to follow? I have managed many teams over the years, and usually, my style of leadership is that of a coach leader: I believe in people's ability to achieve their dreams and want to inspire them.

Since becoming a consultant ten years ago, I have had the pleasure of working with Tiphaine Modeste from Expertise Spa Bien Etre as we developed three seminars in France focused on leadership, retail, and marketing. Whether you are in France, the UK, or anywhere else in the world, leadership is key to growing your perspective and business, and our workshops were so popular that we grew them into modules that were impactful for both owners and managers alike.

As part of the leadership seminar, we had the pleasure of working with Laurent Prieur. Laurent is a disruptor when it comes to thought processes and manages change in companies that need a consultant to handle such impact in large organizations. He now teaches the younger generation to think differently and adapt to change.

When Laurent talks about leadership, he encourages you to think about the song, color, perfume, and tactile feelings that represent leadership to you.

For example, mine are:

→ Song: Don't Stop Me Now by Queen - I just feel so elevated when I sing and dance to this blurring out of my headphones!

→ Colour: It's got to be red. Whenever I have a meeting that I want to impact, I wear red, whether it's a lipstick, a top or a piece of jewellery.

→ Perfume: Chanel No.5 is mine, I feel so empowered when I wear it

→ Tactile: Any silk tops makes me feel like I live in luxury and create a sense of power.

What's Yours?

Think about what empowers you and makes you feel on top of the world. After all, your mindset needs to be protected on a daily basis. Your leadership is also defined by the habits you create and the things that make you feel good and elevated.

I want to share his work with you through an exercise that he shared in the seminar.

Firstly, I want you to take five minutes to answer these 30 questions without thinking too much about them. It's simple: read the question and tick whether:

→ It's me

➜ It's sometimes me

➜ Me? Never

Once you have done that, I will give you further instructions on what to do next. The other columns will be used to evaluate your answers.

Let's go!

Leadership in an Operational Business

	Sentences that suit me	Yes it's totally me	It's sometimes me	me? Never	Directive	Chief	Visionnary	Collaborative	Participative	Coach
1	That's not what I asked!									
2	I am disappointed, I was expecting more from you									
3	As long as there is a good team spirit, we can solve everything									
4	Together, we are more intelligent									
5	The future of our company is you who build it day after day									
6	Do not give up: failure is a rich lesson for tomorrow									
7	We are today ahead of our time and able to meet all challenges									
8	Together we are the best									
9	I don't have all the answers									
10	I can help you see things more clearly, but you will do it alone; I'm sure!									
11	I tried the product last night, here are the errors I found									
12	Did you hear what I tell you?									
13	If he is incompetent, let us separate									
14	Stay united and loyal to each other please									
15	Have I been clear? (angry)									
16	I think it's good to go in that direction but I can be wrong									
17	Our skills are the seeds of our future victories									
18	No problem, I'll resume my tasks later: I'm listening									
19	And you what do you think ?.									
20	I am only the manager of the team									
21	What we are going to accomplish in the next few months is bigger than us.									
22	Do not argue with me									
23	I think you should take this training									
24	How can this take you so much time?									
25	If you need mediation, you can count on me									
26	All ideas are good to take									
27	You have two days to ...									
28	It can't be complicated, show me ...									
29	we will soon become a leader with our products and values.									
30	Yes, your customer welcoming was not perfect, but we will be able to improve it									
31	Nothing beats a brainstorming to imagine new solutions									
32	What do you think you need to do better tomorrow?									
33	You did not play the game: yellow card!									
34	Your work is not bad, but we must continue!									
35	You will do this, then that and you keep me informed.									
36	« I have a dream... »									
	TOTAL									

My main leadership profile is: _____
My secondary leadership profile is: _____
I have to work the leadership profile: _____

Now, let's review your answer...

1: The Directive Leader:

Sofia is the manager of "Spa Terrible," a company in which she is the main decision-maker on a day-to-day basis. Her direct boss gives her flexibility and only gets involved when she thinks it's necessary. In the first year, Sofia managed 30 people who were focused and great at their jobs. Today, she has 125 people under her and continues to manage every single detail of the operation.

She is a true queen of micromanagement!

If you have ticked questions 1, 12, 15, 22, 27, and 35, then add a 1 in the Directive column.

Traits of a Directive Leader:

Sofia needs a lot of information, details, and analysis as she is a micromanager, after all.

➔ Does Sofia need this constant and precise reporting to reassure herself?

➔ Does she feel that she has control over her business?

➔ Does she do this to control her power?

Nobody knows. But what we do know is that she likes to give orders.

The Directive Leader's Consequences:

→ The employees are disempowered

→ Creates a feeling of distrust - "since you are not able to do a good job, I will give you tasks so precise that you will not be able to make mistakes."

→ Kills creativity

→ Generates resistance

What is the Point of Directive Leadership?

→ Absolute need for coherence.

→ The directive leader does not hide flaws or weaknesses.

→ Directive style harms the business climate and sometimes its productivity.

→ Caution... Requires work on self-awareness: reactions, behaviors, tone of voice, which can be difficult for a directive leader.

→ Managing emotions: understanding and managing your own fears, anger, and stress.

→ An irascible directive leader is a little boss nobody wants!

→ Empathy: to get closer to employees, create a connection to be better followed.

→ The directive style combines particularly well with the visionary and participative styles.

→ Visionary to provide meaning and gather around a vision affected by micromanagement.

→ There is a need to develop the participatory aspect of their leadership to promote the involvement and empowerment of everyone.

2: The Chief Leader:

Warning: We'll have to follow him!

Paul runs "Salon Difficult," employing 75 people. This is the third company he manages alone. For him, leadership is above all about setting an example. He is the first to adhere to it to prove that a task is not so difficult. Paul is inexhaustible; he succeeds in everything he does and has trouble understanding that not everyone is as effective or motivated as he is!

Paul is the true chief leader.

If you have ticked questions 2, 11, 13, 24, 28, and 34, then add a 1 in the Chief column.

The Chief Leader's Traits:

The search for excellence and therefore its extreme competence

➜ An example is mentioned here is that of the Italian conductor Arturo Toscanini (1867-1957). He would one day, while conducting an orchestra, decide that the trumpeter was playing badly, and would have taken the trumpet out of his hands to play in his place. In the process, he would have done the same with a violinist, and the musicians would have realized that he surpassed them on all levels. Quote from Toscanini: "Man needs so many masterpieces to feed his mind that he has nothing to do with mediocrity."

➜ Our manager Paul is a little Toscanini of the company. He does better than everyone in his own field.

➜ Impressive, he commands respect and pulls everyone up. Only ... do we want to follow him?

➜ Does he leaves room for mistakes?

➜ How does he react with whom can not follow?

→ Does Paul take the time to congratulate his team when they do a good job?

→ How is the self-esteem of the employees?

→ Losses along the way ... turn-over ... burn-outs

→ He needs a Dream Team: will he be able to recruit them?

The Chief Leader's Consequences:

→ When the team is highly motivated and already competent, the Chief Leader is an effective style that delivers fast results.

→ The team is driven towards greater performance under the guidance of this leader.

→ On the other hand, the Chief Leader shines the brightest with a Dream Team, as they are not faced with incompetence.

→ With a Dream Team - a team that is already operational and motivated - the Chief Leader can relax a little and provide more autonomy to their employees.

What is the Point of the Chief Leadership?

→ The Chief Leader balances with the Visionaries which conveys passion and Collaborative cohesion creator styles.

→ The leader is often admired, without always benefiting from strong leadership skills, but is alone at the top of his pyramid.

→ Beware of perfectionism, it is far from motivating

3: The Visionary Leader:

He inspires you!

It is no longer Sam who runs "Tomorrow Spa." He's not even there anymore, but he's always mentioned. His humor or eloquence was certainly remarkable, but above all, it was his ability to share and inspire an enthusiastic vision of the company's future that made him unique. With him, the mundane aspects of daily work faded away, and you always left feeling energized, looking up at the sky, after his interventions.

If you have ticked questions 5, 7, 17, 21, 29, and 36, then add a 1 in the Visionary column.

. . .

The Visionary Leader's Traits:

➜ No micromanagement, it never even enters their mind…

➜ A desire to "enlist" others in their dream. For example: "Our company has embraced the digital revolution early on, and new customers, such as those in the luxury industry, are turning to us to meet their urgent needs."

➜ Tomorrow, we will be the ones leading innovative programs and technological creativity.

➜ Tomorrow, we will be the ones achieving successful projects and being featured in magazines (etc.).

➜ Working hours, salary, etc. can become secondary considerations compared to the "mission." However, the vision is sincere and aligned.

The Visionary Leader's Consequences:

➜ Dreaming big is great, but in operational businesses, everyday details can be overlooked.

➜ The lack of day-to-day direction.

➜ Increase in frustration.

➜ A team that does what they want and says what they think the leader wants to hear to motivate them.

➜ Risk: using language and concepts that are incomprehensible to most people.

What is the Point of the Visionary Leadership?

➜ Imperative: to control the quality of the directives.

➜ May well be combined with a Directive style, which will be medium-dose supported thanks to its charisma and inspired inspiration.

➜ Very positive for the atmosphere in the company and the motivation. The key: his managers to create and implement his dreams.

4: The Collaborative Leader:

Unity is strength, and harmony makes everything possible.

Jack has been leading his team at "Salon Together" for three years. The company values are strong and emphasized on a daily basis, but what truly binds Jack's team together is not just a sense of belonging to the company. It is rather his leadership, which is focused on collaboration. He actively seeks harmony within his team and intervenes as soon as conflicts arise. He always makes sure to address each team member, leaving no one behind. He frequently organizes team lunches, cultural events, or sports outings to foster unity among his team.

His main concern is ensuring that everyone feels integrated and connected to one another.

If you have ticked questions 3, 8, 14, 20, 25, and 33, then add a 1 in the Collaborative column.

The Collaborative Leader's Traits:

➔ Collective play: cohesion, unity ... equality

➔ Objective: to make each other work "hand in hand"

➔ Soothes conflicts

➔ Exchange meetings are regular, during or outside working hours.

➔ He is perceived as empathetic, understanding, human and inspires confidence.

The Collaborative Leader's Consequences:

→ He tracks the "flossy"

→ "I am not a number!" is in his vocabulary

→ Dissolving the feeling of uniqueness in the face of unity: potential demotivation of individual

→ Uniform syndrome, and little "personal reward"

→ Unable to deal with "divas"

What is the Point of the Collaborative Leadership?

→ Style unsuitable for over-performing employees

→ Ineffective style in times of crisis or requiring an emergency

→ Ideal for easing tensions in a team, supporting motivation in difficult times (restructuring, merger, decline or peak activity)

→ Collaborative style proves relevant in addition to other styles as a main component

5: The Participative Leader:

Never a single race, long live collective intelligence!

Dialogue, consensus, and democracy: When Carole took over the company, she noticed that her predecessor had caused frustrations among the staff. Many employees had made suggestions but were never heard. Persistent issues such as unbalanced schedules and dissatisfied customers remained unresolved. The teams had solutions to propose, but they felt tired of their proposals falling on deaf ears.

Carole, on the other hand, is a leader who embraces a resolutely democratic approach. She listens attentively and values the input of her teams.

If you have ticked questions 4, 9, 16, 19, 26, and 31, then add a 1 in the Participative column.

The Participative Leader's Traits:

→ Popular voice: the path of collective intelligence

→ Like the collaborative, this leader puts the people before the tasks.

→ Open-mindedness and good listening skills that capture all the values produced by teams

➜ Big advantage: everything does not depend on her alone

➜ Very positive for the climate of the company which then benefits from a strong implication.

The Participative Leader's Consequences:

➜ Promotes collective creativity and innovation.

➜ This style is optimal for: obtaining unanimity or commitment, and collecting valuable ideas from employees (for example, if you are a new manager of a team that knows more than you!).

➜ She finds the right path when the leader needs the creativity of her teams/colleagues.

➜ In addition to situational intelligence, the leader has every interest in adapting her style to the personalities around her. "High performers" (very competent and excellent employees) may become impatient if they have to wait for the next day to seek the community's opinion to move forward.

What is the Point of the Participative Leadership?

→ To find the right path when she is uncertain, to encourage engagement and collect good ideas.

→ This style of leadership is less relevant when there is a need to make quick and decisive decisions and obtain rapid results. It is also unsuitable in times of crisis.

→ Even on a daily basis, this leader needs to know how to conclude the discussions she initiated, which means saying, "Okay, I've heard you, but now it's my turn to make the decision."

→ To fully benefit from this wealth of collective intelligence, this democratic leader must also know how to make decisions and remember that she is the leader.

→ With certain personalities, the leader succeeds by being less participative and drawing inspiration from the directive or commanding style.

6: The Coach Leader:

Paradoxical style, guiding without giving direct instructions! Active listening & master of feedback: it takes you beyond yourself...

Beatrice prefers working with small teams, especially the one she currently leads. Throughout her career, she has been fortunate to come across individuals in whom she believes. Is it luck? She recognizes their weaknesses and vulnerabilities, but above all, she sees immense potential for growth in each member of her team.

Every day, she engages in listening, communication, support, and guidance to help each team member develop their skills.

If you have ticked questions 6, 10, 18, 23, 30, and 32, then add a 1 in the Coach column.

The Coach Leader's Traits:

→ This leader believes in you and invests in you.

→ The purpose of this leadership is to align your goals with those of the company.

→ She aims to highlight your talents and help you improve.

→ What displeases this leader is stagnation, wasted talent, and disengagement.

→ Yet, this is the style that most encourages intrinsic motivation, as the leader actively seeks to bring it out and connect it to the company's objectives. It's as if the coach-like leader invites everyone to be a visionary for themselves and then creates connections between their vision and the company's goals.

> No matter how much time you spend thinking about, worrying about, focusing on, questioning the value of, and evaluating people, it won't be enough.... People are the only thing that matters, and the only thing you should think about, because when that part is right, everything else works. - David Ogilvy

The Coach Leader's Consequences:

→ The effects on the team and atmosphere are highly positive, as everyone feels valued and supported. Beyond individual growth, the "Coach" leader focuses on building competent teams.

→ It's a delicate art that requires a significant amount of time, which means that the impact on the team may be slow at times.

→ It's impossible to achieve with a chief or directive leader, as they may not understand or appreciate the coaching style of leadership.

➔ The coaching style is ideal for motivated team members seeking personal growth and development.

➔ However, it may not be suitable for employees with little autonomy or those who are not interested in taking on responsibilities.

➔ Another challenge is knowing how to establish clear and effective boundaries.

What is the Point of Coach Leadership?

➔ The "Coach" leader should have a clear understanding of their role and expectations for their team in terms of communication and exchange.

➔ Emotional intelligence skills are crucial for the coaching leader, including the ability to develop others, emotional awareness, and empathy.

➔ The coaching style is not effective for achieving quick results or molding employees into a predefined mold. For these purposes, a chief or directive leader is more effective.

Now, it's time for you to add your scores at the bottom of the sheet:

	Directive	Chief	Visionary	Collaborative	Participative	Coach
TOTAL						

My main leadership profile is: _____
My secondary leadership profile is: _____
I have to work the leadership profile: _____

Recap

1. The Directive Leader: "Do as I tell you." Directive leaders prioritize results and can be intimidating, often pushing their teams to reach targets at all costs. While they can deliver quick results, this leadership style can damage the work atmosphere and productivity. Directive leaders rarely show vulnerability, leading to a sense of isolation.

2. The Chief Leader: "Do it now." Chief leaders strive for excellence and command respect through their strong expectations. While their drive for immediate action can be productive, they may overlook individual perspectives, making employees feel undervalued. Prolonged use of this leadership style can lead to high staff turnover.

3. The Visionary Leader: "Come build the dream with me." Visionary leaders inspire and create a positive atmosphere that motivates people. However, they can be weak in managing the operational aspects of the business and may overlook day-to-day details.

4. The Collaborative Leader: "Together we are stronger." Collaborative leaders focus on fostering teamwork and resolving conflicts. They involve everyone in the business's activities and are perceived as empathetic and inspirational. However, they may spend excessive time listening rather than taking action, which can hinder achieving fast results.

5. The Participative Leader: "What do you think?" Participative leaders value each individual's input and encourage team commitment. While they gather ideas and make team members feel valued, their decision-making process can be slow, and they may be seen as indecisive. This leadership style may face challenges in times of crisis, requiring the leader to make decisive choices.

6. The Coach Leader: "Try this." Coach leaders invest in individuals, highlighting their talents and promoting self-improvement. They are well-suited for ambitious team members, but they expect engagement and a willingness to take responsibility. Coach leaders possess high emotional intelligence, demonstrating empathy and supporting team members' development. However, the coaching style may not be effective for achieving quick team accomplishments.

Adapt For Success

When it comes to adapting your style of leadership, I wanted to share this experience with you of the Spa I mentioned earlier and how it enabled me to redefine my leadership through experiences I had with my career so far and bring this Spa back to life.

I was traveling a lot with this company, and since they had decided to stay within the retail side of the business, I realized that I needed to revisit my direction as I love retail but was missing the service element for the customer journey to feel complete.

I was looking after several boutiques and had to reach targets by empowering the teams with clear and defined leadership, which was a priority alongside the day-to-day management and strategy for growth. I was missing working with therapists and the whole dimension that a Spa would bring to my role.

I had a recruiter that followed me through my career, even found me some roles, so every now and then, he would call to introduce me to a new shiny role or ask me if I knew of anyone. I liked him; he made it personal, and we always had a good catch up, putting the world at peace.

On one of the calls, I explained where I was in my career. I had moved to this company hoping to become a group spa director; instead, I was traveling to support the boutiques and ensure we delivered all of the details that this corporation was expecting.

"Valerie, I have the perfect role for you. It's a spa that is in need of strong leadership. You have the right profile; it's got potential, and it's 30 minutes away from your home (which in London is a bonus!)" He went on about the role, and when I discovered which he was talking about, I cut him off: "Absolutely no way, it has a terrible reputation, and on top of that, there is a dragon in charge. I will never be interested."

The hair and beauty industry is a small one, even in a big city like London; you know who has moved where, and you know the reputation of the place. It's incredible how words and actions travel quickly.

Fast forward three months later, he calls me and mentions that they still were unable to find anyone, that I would be perfect for the role, blah blah blah but I thought to myself, I'm not surprised! No one wants it!

Having had a small car accident and feeling like I was going nowhere with my role, I agreed to an interview. I met my dragon and the HR director, came back for a second interview with a presentation of what I would do to bring it back to the brink of success. I had it in the bag, I felt, I thought, how bad can it be?

I quickly understood that, besides the towels or the therapists wishing me good luck in my journey since I was the 9th manager in nine years (hard to get over that one!!), the spa structure and communication were inefficient. The team had the upper hand on everything that was done and implemented. In particular, the team that generated the most revenue called the shots. Everything they wanted was granted, and their influence was pretty impressive.

While I love listening to the team and believe that communication needs to flow both ways for a business to thrive, I also understand that in an operational business, the structure must be right for everything to flow smoothly. The systems in place should promote a smooth flow so that everyone knows the impact that their role has on the day-to-day operations.

As a coach, I could adopt my leadership style while working with corporates, as there are more layers of management to support me, and I have the time to grow my teams. However, in this smaller business, even though the revenue is impressive, we are all under one roof, and every detail of what we do, feel, and breathe has an impact on the day and, therefore, on the customer journey. I quickly realized that coaching a lot of people would be a huge challenge, and if I did, I would waste a lot of time.

In the three weeks of observing, I saw some shocking horror that was detrimental to the business and the ethos of the company. I said nothing and just sat there in disbelief that the team could have such an impact on the running of the place. To the extent that the reception team was bullied and suffering, some were even leaving on Prozac after just three months of working in what I could only describe as a toxic environment. I was told, "Valerie, it's quiet at the moment, but wait till September. They're all going to come back, and we're going to make so much money." Well, September came, and it was busier, but not to the extent they had mentioned. It was never to the stage where we could bring ourselves back from the brink.

As a single mother of two young children, failure was not an option. Not only that, but it would also look terrible on my resume, and my pride was poked by this sense of wanting to succeed. So I centered my thoughts and decided that my leadership style had to change, or

I would be the 9th manager in nine years, and that was impossible to even contemplate.

I had a vision that not only would I have a cake with a candle that both this therapist and I would blow as I would be the only manager that has managed to stay over 1 year, but I would also bring this spa back to life. I would change the operation so it would be more coherent, less toxic, and far more enjoyable. I pulled my sleeve up and started working on my vision, strategy, and overall operational details that it needed. This spa needed me to be a directive and chief leader to gain respect; otherwise, I would be eaten alive in this tiger's den.

I had to manage my dragon too; her expectations had to be met, and I had to ensure that I could focus on each staff performance, rebalance the communication, and ensure everyone knew their roles. It was completely against my nature to change my style of leadership; never in my career had I had to become such a leader. Of course, I had to have firm conversations and have a reputation for being strict and direct, but never to that extent. As a Coach leader, I had a lot of time for people who wanted to learn and explore their strength and found it difficult to support lazy or unbothered staff. To me, if you are going to do a job, do it well, even if it's a part-time role in something that will never be for the long term; your attitude towards it is what makes it bearable and enjoyable in the moment. Otherwise, why bother?!

I know that I can turn around any mindset to my way of thinking and coach my teams so far to follow me in my vision by being so focused on them and their visions. I had successfully turned around mindsets and set the teams up for success. If in any case, my previous bosses wanted me to deal with difficult teams and lack of achieving targets because they knew I could turn them around. But as mentioned, in a corporate world, you do have more support around you, so my style of coaching was strong enough to motivate and create individual focuses that change the dynamic of the team and impacts on the customer journey. In this instance, it was very different as I had to manage my boss and her expectations, but I was also in a small environment, living, breathing, and being part of the day-to-day. It felt that if I was unable to change what was going on quickly and fast, I would lose all respect of the team.

My dragon was dismissed after two months of me being there, so suddenly I could be a lot more impactful in the way I wanted to do things, but in the meantime, after my three weeks of observations, I had a meeting with them and laid down the law: this is what I have seen, and this is what we are going to do from now on. I made it clear, I was the directive and chief leader, and if someone didn't want to work with me, the door was opened. I went as far as giving them 10 minutes to make up their mind and went downstairs (was breathing in a bag thinking omg what have I done, I am going to go up and everyone will be gone!). By the time I came back up, no one had left. So I carried on with: ok, so this means you will agree with what I want to do here from now on, and anyone who goes against it will go directly on disciplinary in the view to be dismissed.

I was out of my comfort zone, but I knew that my strategy was right. I knew what to do to bring the spa back to life and overcome everything. My sole mission was to be the first manager to stay for over a year, and my mission was so clear that I told everyone who wanted to hear it.

After that meeting, I did dismiss a couple of hard-core employees, and my first mission was to recruit fresh talent with a new mindset to bring another dimension to the team dynamic.

I realized that being directive and chief was never a long-term strategy, as it could demotivate the team in the long run and be counterproductive to empowering them. It was also against my leadership style!

So my visionary leadership came out quickly, especially for the newcomers, so they could follow my dream. I created five mantras for the team to follow, and I made sure everyone heard them. The more dreamy I was, the more I could empower everyone around me.

My mantra was as follows, and I still remember it to this day as it was part of my core message:

Five Key Mantras to Follow

1. Achieving targets for the year by focusing on each client and creating a 5-star customer journey that will make everyone want to come back.
2. Individual and team meetings are a priority, and communication is the most important aspect of our day-to-day operations.
3. Create a strong marketing and networking strategy to bring the buzz back into the spa.
4. Deliver a strong management and reception team that is efficient and focused on their targets.
5. Ensure that the treatment and retail sales are incredible for each client so that they want to come back again and again.

Your vision can be as such, or it can be very much a sentence that is clear and concise. We will revisit this in this book. Then, the collaborative and participative leadership hat came to the limelight, and my priority was individual and team meetings. I got interested in every single one of them, putting out fires and drama that occurred on a day-to-day basis for two months. I created strong individual plans to empower each of them.

Only then could I be the coach that I loved and was natural to me. By then, I had them where I wanted them. Each knew their place, my expectations, and were empowered to achieve the global vision. The spa needed refurbishment, and everything was falling apart, but since we had no budget, the only thing I had was to keep them focused with a military operation (chief and directive) with clear processes. I shared my clear vision with everyone who talked to me (visionary), had my meetings on an individual and team meeting (collaborative and participative), and my coaching program ensured that each of my staff felt they belonged to something strong, and their voice and career mattered (coach).

In six months, we were achieving figures exceeding last year's, and in on year, we were exceeding our target, which had never been seen before. The only thing I focused on was the mindset of each team member, ensuring that communication was two-way and never toxic, which was the key to success.

My reputation grew as a strict manager, which I didn't mind, but I knew it was far from the truth. I was consistent, meaning that I did what I said and said what I did, so there were always clear intentions and defined structure.

I knew that I would attract the right candidates who wanted to work with me, while the others, Flossy or wannabe Flossy, would never last too long. I became a perfectionist regarding my intentions and the standards I wanted to deliver, but I was aware that perfectionism could go against empowering others. Therefore, I remained flexible enough to adapt to situations and revert to business needs all the time.

I understood that by coaching everyone, especially the managers, I could then go out and network, grow the business's reputation, and ensure that every detail of the customer journey mattered. I learned through customer feedback what was right for our clientele and what needed improvement. The focus on employees and customers was at the heart of our conversations so that we could grow together and showcase what a great team we had become.

In all, to be a successful leader, you need to be adaptable and able to use different leadership styles at different points. Directive and chief leadership styles are, as you can see, far from ideal for motivating teams to stay with you in the long run but are necessary at times. For Marc and Marie, it becomes apparent that the Chief & Directive leadership style is their preferred approach, and they are unable to accept anything else as they are completely in love with what they are generating in terms of their leadership. So, learning about leadership becomes more and more important and crucial to define what we do and achieve that vision. Once you know your leadership style, you can then nurture the other styles to feel complete and overcome all situations.

Confession Time!

Marc found it difficult to find a multisite manager and although he craved the support, he was constantly advertising to alleviate his pressure. During the recruitment process, I asked him what he was doing and he revealed that every time he had a potential candidate, he would send them a three-month plan of everything that he wanted them to do, including dates and times of meetings as well as where they would spend their time and what reports needed to be sent.

When hiring senior staff, trust must be there for them to do their work. Was he ready for such a person? The idea of empowering his existing managers never came to his mind, or even developing one of them into a multisite manager. Sometimes the fear of change makes you look at things the way you want them, but looking at his structure and individual development plan was the only way forward, as at least his managers were used to his ways!

The Soft Skills of Leadership and What Are They For?

When becoming the leader you have always dreamt of, it's crucial to develop your soft skills in order to overcome every situation that is thrown at you. We can put systems in place and become operationally smooth, but sometimes situations occur, and that's when your soft skills come to light. I saw that the successful members who stayed with me throughout the pandemic were very adaptable in their mindset and understood what it took to grow and everything they needed to do in order to save the business. These leaders thrived through adversity because of their way of behaving and empowering their teams. Their soft skills grew in coaching, and their vision, although blurry at the beginning, became clearer.

Soft skills are most of the time unnoticed. We know how we work, but sometimes, we are unaware that this is a strength. For example, when Marie in all her glory of being a micro-manager decided to do something, her decisiveness is clearly a soft skill. Albeit, it is decisions that rely purely on her workload, however, channelled properly and with the right structure, it could be even more powerful.

By definition, soft skills are personal attributes that enable someone to interact effectively and harmoniously with other people.

As far as I am concerned, soft skills are great for decision making but also promote a healthy work environment as well as efficiency in the business. They can also drive individuals to overcome emotions. Developing and understanding your soft skills will make you complete as a leader. When I told my mother that I teach time management and organizational structure, she was laughing! Perhaps because she remembers me as the messy, never caring about time teenager! And I was. Thanks to some amazing managers, I refined my way and learnt (sometimes the hard way) how I could impact others even more through some key soft skills. My communication, for example, as a French woman in the UK could be perceived as extremely direct, and when I learnt that I would come across too harshly to function this way in an English market, I learnt so much about communication that it became a strength.

To me, soft skills improve retention of your employees in your business. Why is it that some employees remain with you when other similar roles pay higher? Because it's more than the money. Employees value being valued and search for that place where they are respected, and only your structure, organization, and soft skills can make them feel that way. I am being generic, but it is important that your values align with your soft skills.

We are all leaders, and we can learn skills that will empower us to do better and even thrive in some situations. But most of all, these skills will enable you to keep your mindset fresh and strong. Having gone through a lot on a personal level, I will never be the one to advocate that you must think positive! I think that can be a huge pressure in itself. But nurturing the cognitive thought process of your mind and your soft skills will be what will make you feel better. And if you feel better, you attract better things, people, and situations around you, one step at a time. I am a huge fan of Neuro-Linguistic Programming Therapy, which my mum introduced me to when I was young, and still love that thought process.

You will find that focusing on too many soft skills at once will be overwhelming and you may revert to old habits very quickly. However, creating a strong plan of action for yourself will keep you aligned with your goals, and your mindset will become stronger as you progress. Little steps can make a huge difference in the end. For example, when I learned time management, I focused on that for a whole year and it became a habit that I continue to improve even now. When I was told about my communication style, I focused on that for a year to learn how to empower others with better channels of communication. Some soft skills may take less time to master, but focusing on them will only strengthen your mindset and skills.

I strongly believe that developing soft skills will make you more efficient in your work and create a sense of achievement, which in itself is powerful.

There are many soft skills that you can work on, but these are the ones I believe are crucial to your growth:

→ SELF MOTIVATION

I deal with a lot of burnt-out leaders, and to tell them to become positive in my eyes is completely counterproductive. Instead, we focus on the way they talk to themselves. A long time ago, I listened to this podcast (I wish I could remember which one that was; I failed to write it down!), but she mentioned that for three weeks, whenever you are aware of your thoughts (as we have so many we are unconscious of), have a little notepad and pen in your bag/pocket and write them down, especially thoughts about yourself. I did it for the three weeks, and when I reverted back to it, it was so disturbing how I spoke to myself. Words that I would never even say to my worst enemy, words that could destroy any mindset from the get-go, let alone the subconscious thoughts I was not even aware of! It was no longer serving me, and I did everything in my power to change the way I viewed myself, starting by respecting my image, my being, rather than putting myself down in every avenue. I started celebrating the wins rather than highlighting what I failed to do or was far from being great at. I started focusing on loving my way of being, and although a slow process, it allowed me to become more motivated and aligned with my vision. I could actually see that vision rather than it being blocked by so many self-beliefs that it empowered me. Most of the time, when I work with clients, I can see that self-motivation can be up and down: one day great, one day awful. Instead of using that language - awful, difficult, unfair, not good enough - we simply change the language to: I had a challenging week/day, I did that instead. Self-sabotage is your own worst enemy when it comes to self-motivation.

→ RESPONSIBILITY

Understanding that ultimately what you put out there will come back to you and become responsible for your actions or non actions for that matter, will allow you to create stronger relationships with everyone around you. Being responsible for you own values, mindset and results, you will find that you become stronger as a leader and accepting defeat or change will ultimately make you more flexible which is such a strength. I was always the first one to say when I messed something up and admit it to my team: "ok, on this one, it was a poor decision, I found this solution instead:, let's create best practice and move forward." Admitting made me more respected and more human. As we are dealing with people, being able to have that responsible mindset allows you to create strong bonds and reassures the team. In the past, I dealt with difficult bosses and by taking the full responsibility of my team, they felt protected and lead. That is such a powerful way to behave and will gain you commitment from the team.

→ TEAMWORK

If you're going to work with people, you have to love them! Otherwise, you might be in the wrong job. Teamwork is essential for any business, and enjoying the buzz of it is crucial for any aspiring leader. I remember working for a corporation that made every single person in the office work on the shop floor during Christmas. They wanted to ensure that everyone knew what was happening on the ground and could make practical decisions for all accounts, rather than being safe in the office and making impractical decisions. This was a brilliant idea! When was the last time you worked on the floor? And if you did, did you enjoy it? If you didn't, why not? Working on the floor can highlight real issues, and by addressing them, you can make practical decisions that will gain the team's respect. No job is too small, and team members will appreciate you even more for getting your hands dirty alongside them.

Teamwork is also highlighted in the way you conduct individual and team meetings, as well as how you empower the team via team-building days. It's also about communication and smooth operation that will encapsulate your standards. I used to love working at reception every now and then, as you can see so much from there. After a while, everyone forgets that you are there, and the true culture of the team spirit comes out. Have you ever been somewhere as a customer and thought that the service was exceptional? I remember going to a bank that had just undergone a refurbishment, and I was blown away by their service! A gentleman standing there greeted me and asked how I was. He then asked me what I wanted to do at the bank today. I said I wanted to deposit a check. He asked for my bank card, realized that I was a premium member, smiled, and showed me to the counter I needed to go to. I arrived at the counter, and the lady behind the glass smiled and said, "Welcome Miss Delforge, how are you today?" I was puzzled about how she knew my name already, and the whole experience felt so personalized. Then I realized she had a little headset in her ear, and so did he. He must have mentioned "Miss Delforge with a red scarf on." That attention to detail in the operation and customer journey was no accident. It took a leader to decide how to welcome the client, individuals to execute it well, and a team effort to bring it alive. Team effort becomes the culture of the business, which reflects on the customer journey and ultimately brings you loyalty. No expensive stuff or investment is ever needed as much as you think. It's all about the team and your perception of your business.

➜ PROBLEM SOLVING

That can be a difficult one as for our Marc and Marie out there, it's possibly giving them a lot of anxiety. Problem-solving is always about a rounded approach to the issue, but when we are in the midst of things, we tend to only think of one solution and run with it. Reflection on the issue is key to ensure that the solution is the most impactful one. So, problem-solving becomes a soft skill that allows you to have a better approach to challenges.

I love looking at a problem and flipping it on its head, even thinking of solutions that I perhaps would never consider. But it's about the business, the team, and the customers, so ultimately my perception could be wrong. I have to look at it from all angles. The anxiety that problem-solving brings is purely down to the fear of failure, sometimes the fear of success, that creates awful feelings.

However, if you make a decision, stand by it, let it grow, and most of all, revisit it to ensure it has had the best possible outcome. As a leader, once more, to be wrong and admit it is better than to be stubborn and stick to something that has a negative effect. Problem-solving is best when you give yourself time, but we do have to react to something quickly sometimes, which is why I believe in procedures so much. They allow you to have a base for those decisions. Revisiting them and talking through them will be the most rewarding, as you will constantly learn from them.

→ DECISIVENESS

Being decisive comes with the territory as a leader, and I believe that's where micromanagement can really take over. I also believe that there is always a solution to the issues that are presented in front of you, and there are no right or wrong decisions. Once you have analyzed the situation, thought through the potential outcomes, and believe you are making the right decision, you should commit to it and never let go. Decisiveness means committing to that solution, and it is essential to review and follow up to ensure those commitments are working towards the best possible outcomes. Perhaps you need to tweak your decision slightly or revisit some of the processes. It's important that once you make that choice, you believe it is the right one. If you keep changing your mind, you will not only lose the interest of those who follow you, but you will also live in a constant state of indecisiveness, which will destroy any kind of leadership you are trying to build in your business. Decision-making goes hand in hand with your business direction, and unless you know where you are going, you will make on-the-spot decisions or simply float around, which will make the growth of your business plateau or even become unstable.

→ WORK UNDER PRESSURE

One could argue that the moment you become an owner, you work under pressure constantly and therefore, it is a skill that you have acquired by default. It's also strange when we have a client telling us that they work best under pressure. It's as if they thrive on everyone pulling together, wanting to overcome what is happening in the day. Why can't it be like that all of the time? To me, that can be a healthy pressure and a sign of a good team. Sometimes you just have to pull the team up. It would be interesting for you to notice what you do that is so different from the "normal" days. I think that when working under pressure, communication is clearer and everyone knows what they need to do. But working under pressure when you are a micromanager is another level of pressure because of the psychological aspect of control and having everything your way. If you can start working, trusting your processes and your team, as well as delegating the day ahead without constant worry, you might find that you are starting to grow your leadership skills and starting to dilute your micromanagement.

→ NEGOTATION

Negotiation is vital to resolving differences in opinion, challenges in the workplace, or growing the business to the best of your abilities by gaining the best for the business. Negotiation skills involve getting a win-win outcome for both parties, but as a micromanager, it can be challenging to achieve this since you may be too deep into the day-to-day. Being emotionally adept allows negotiations to run smoothly and generate an overall business strategy, but this can be difficult for micromanagers who struggle to respond to the emotions of others. Learning negotiation skills can feel uncomfortable as it may require stepping outside of your comfort zone. However, finding your style of negotiation is key to developing your skills. I believe that to negotiate effectively, you must actively listen and have a constant solution-finding mindset, which micro-managers may find challenging.

➜ CONFLICT RESOLUTION

This is similar to negotiation skills but specific to conflicts. Micro-managers can find it very difficult to work on this skill as they may see conflicts in a one-sided way. Developing collaborative leadership skills is key to resolving conflict, and patience and processes are important to focus on. Conflict is a normal, and even healthy, part of relationships. After all, it is natural for two people to sometimes disagree, especially within a team where there may be clashes of personalities. Since relationship conflicts are inevitable, learning to deal with them in a healthy way is crucial.

When conflict is mismanaged, it can harm the relationship. But when handled in a respectful and positive way, conflict provides an opportunity for growth, ultimately strengthening the bond between two people. By learning the skills needed for successful conflict resolution, you can keep your personal and professional relationships strong and growing. However, this can be the biggest challenge for micro-managers such as Marc and Marie.

→ INTEGRITY

It can be difficult to understand why integrity is considered a skill, as being integral to your team, business, and yourself should be something that comes naturally. However, in my experience coaching many business owners, I have come to realize that integrity can sometimes be lost in the midst of day-to-day operations. Leaders with integrity are honest, trustworthy, and reliable. They say what they mean and mean what they say, and they own up to their mistakes. This can be challenging for micro-managers who often have a rigid way of doing things and may struggle to admit when they are wrong. It is not uncommon for micro-managers like Marc and Marie to blame their teams for any shortcomings rather than taking responsibility themselves. However, creating a culture of integrity is essential to creating a sense of belonging and direction for everyone on the team. When leaders show integrity, they inspire their teams to embody the true ethos of the company and work towards a common goal.

Confession Time!

Marie decided to bring in a new brand that, in her mind, was going to set her apart and differentiate her business from others. She contacted the supplier and began the process, but soon realized that only one of her therapists was willing and able to carry out the treatment, while the others were less than enthusiastic. Despite having already spent over £4,000 on the opening order and committing to a payment plan of £580 per month for the machine required, as well as training for everyone, the brand failed to generate much interest or revenue, and was ultimately shelved after a few Instagram posts. Six months later, it was clear that the brand had been far from profitable, and had actually confused the customer journey as it was too similar to a brand that Marie had been working with for over 5 years. This "my way or no way" type of management and strategy had completely backfired, leaving Marie feeling disgruntled and with a team that would never voice their opinions but whose actions spoke louder than words.

The Most Impactful Soft Skills

➜ TIME MANAGEMENT

Time management is perhaps the most difficult soft skill to master and yet the most important. It's always about time: "I don't have the time", "I try and it comes back to what it was", "I am too busy", "I have so much to do", "no one can do what I do", etc.

So why is time management the trickiest soft skill to develop for entrepreneurs? Because we always go back to what feels comfortable, and because life happens out of our control, bad habits still flourish.

It is the first thing I focus on with my members at the beginning of their journey with us. Master your time and you will instantly feel better. The better you feel, the more successful you will feel, which will impact absolutely everything. I will repeat this message again and again as it is so important to your mindset.

Time management, to me, creates a healthy routine for your workload and enables you to handle everything in a calm manner. When you are writing it down, it's always more manageable than if it's in your head. It allows you to see your business with less emotion and balance your personal life without feeling guilty.

It fascinates me why we find it hard making time for things that matter, and although I mastered it early in my career, I still look into it. I think it's important to review, read and get opinions from different people so you can ensure your system is still correct, or you can tweak it with some new knowledge. Just like the system I am going to give you now, you will make it your own, but there are some key aspects of it that will be non-negotiable, as I have learned throughout the years that they are the key to successful time management.

We all want more time, but this can seem like an impossible goal to achieve. Chances are you have more than one to-do list, and you view every job as a priority but are unable to focus on any one individual task. Quite often, it becomes difficult to assess which is our top priority, and we spend much of our valuable time procrastinating to avoid those dreaded little chores. We become overwhelmed with work, find ourselves going around in circles, and never really get anywhere, always dealing with the same issues. It's a vicious circle. You may have even come across that newfangled, life-changing, miracle-inducing app that will surely do everything for you! But still, I can see a lot of people finding it hard to feel aligned with time management.

There are so many tools and techniques out there claiming to help you, but these can just result in adding to the confusion. We are unable to decide which of these solutions are the answer or adhere to what we think is best, do not follow through, and fall back into old habits because old habits die hard.

Adding to all of this is the constant information we have that can create that guilty feeling of should have, could have, would have. It simply becomes too much, and procrastination can happen faster than you have time to say "Time Management!"

One of my friends who did my time management program sent me an article saying that Steve Jobs never believes in time management and has zero to-do list. I replied saying that I bet he has 15 people around him listening to his every word and they have a to-do list to manage. So until you are Steve Jobs, you will have to manage and work on your to-do list! Fair point she replied, and now structured, is managing various projects at a time with ease.

I have read fantastic books such as 'The Pareto Principle: 80/20 Rule' by Richard Koch and am currently reading 'The 1 Thing' by Gary Keller, which are amazing insights into what we want and what we should strive towards. 'The 4-Hour Work Week' by Tim Ferriss, as well. They are just all brilliant.

But here is the thing: when we are an entrepreneur and especially when we deal with teams and/or customers, that is just adding to the guilt of what we should be doing.

I gave a talk one day on Time Management. One of the attendees sent me an email and said that she felt so motivated by it that evening she revisited her to-do list and priorities. However, she got to work in the morning, and one of her top hairdressers handed her notice, and the water wasn't working correctly, so she had to lose the couple of hours worth of clients, which in itself is a loss that adds to the financial pressure she was already feeling. How can she carry on being on top of her to-do list and motivated when she has to deal with everything else, but feelings that are constantly putting her down? I agree.

Just like the books I just mentioned, I love them and really respect everything they are saying. I took some bits from them to reassess what I do, especially on my one thing, which, as I am writing this book, is precisely my focus. But of course, it is difficult to dismiss everything else I am working on, my team, and clients who all rely on me to provide a service. It's simply a matter of refining my time management and making it function so that the one thing I can focus on remains a priority for the months I have set myself to achieve it by.

But here is the BUT: the minute you are dealing with a business that manages people or clients, your time is no longer entirely your own. How many times have I had to talk to salon owners about managing their diaries and not letting clients dictate their schedules? If you've stated that you're closing at 7pm, why allow a client to demand a waxing appointment at 8pm? Are we afraid of losing money or are we simply unable to stop people-pleasing? No one should be dictating your time, but we often let it happen. Friends, family, and occasions can all become overwhelming.

I've had many debates about time management, especially when someone tells me it's impossible to feel on top of their to-do list because they're constantly falling behind.

I get it, it's a lot to revisit and focus on. It can be something we know we have to do but keep putting off. It's easier to keep our heads in the sand, like the ostrich, than face the reality of managing our time.

To me, it goes down to two key elements:

→ Your structure which we will revisit in this book at a later stage

→ You actually take time to make time for time management, which is a non-negotiable in any way, shape, and form!

Time management is a skill that can be learned, and with a strong focus on developing these skills, it can change your mindset and perspective towards your business. As someone who has managed large teams, I know firsthand the importance of creating clear and precise procedures to help focus and streamline tasks that require full concentration.

There is no magic wand or special potion to master time management, just the knowledge and experience gained from years of running my own company, managing multinational teams, consulting, and balancing my home and family life. All you need to do is engage with the knowledge I am sharing and determine what strategies work best for your unique situation.

Here is my story…

When I was given my first area manager job, I wanted to impress. This was a maternity cover role, and my aim was simple: achieve targets by focusing on the leadership of each team so they would want to keep me in a permanent area management role. I really felt this was my calling, as I had done well in my roles as manager of the brand's counters in various department stores. I overachieved my targets and had most of my team promoted, as I was teaching them as much as I could to keep them motivated. My boss was impressed and gave me a chance to prove myself with an area management role. I was extremely career-minded and had one thing on my mind: learn and progress. Suddenly, with this new role, I had 22 accounts over a specific area to look after, which meant I had to travel a fair amount on a daily basis. In addition to ensuring I reached the overall targets, I had to ensure the processes and standards were met at all times.

Time management was taught in the way of a 12 week Journey Planner which allowed us to structure our workload:

Leadership in an Operational Business

	JANUARY	FEBRUARY	MARCH
1			
2			
3			
4			
5			
6			
7			
8			
9			
10			
11			
12			
13			
14			
15			
16			
17			
18			
19			
20			
21			
22			
23			
24			
25			
26			
27			
28			
29			
30			
31			

In the 12 weeks we were expected to:

→ Visit the high money driven accounts twice in the planner

→ Visit the smaller ones once in the planner

→ Organise four recruitment days

→ Admin day every Monday with clear directives on what was expected

→ Generate new business and visit potential clients six times in the planner

→ Leave yourself four days for moving things around if needed

. . .

Basically, it was all very organised and I loved it! It allowed me to understand my priorities and have a strong system to follow.

Until, that is, the workload came under the spotlight with the amount of work you had to do (they loved paperwork and the cloud system at the time was non-existent, we used to fax, just to give you a perspective on things!). Or if you went on holiday, of course, you still had to deliver. So at times, time management felt a little heavy. When you have to come home after an eight-hour shift and four hours of travel in a day, and do at least one hour of follow-up email, it was a lot on your plate. I guess that as the newbie in this role, it was also important for me to make that impression so I was probably ensuring I was efficient, so I was putting pressure on myself too.

But my memory of time management and what I thought was organized came into disrepute when one day, I realized that having a sudden issue was far from being planned, and it threw everything up in the air. Now, what I learned from it is that if you have zero structure to fall back on, you will be forever lost in direction. Having a structure and system to follow puts everything back into some kind of order, especially in an operational business.

But most of all, I learned that your leadership skills are tested at any point, and you are completely unaware of it.

I had to present to this buyer of a renowned department store the whole of the Christmas collection and get in the orders that she wanted to place. It's called sell-in, and of course, that was part of my target. The other part was to ensure that we sell-through, and that's by focusing the team to sell as much as possible.

This buyer is also renowned to be a nightmare to pin down and get an appointment from her. She knows she needs to see me; I am one of her biggest brands, but it's on her own terms, she decides when it suits her. It's when I started feeling a little anxious as I knew that whenever she gave me an appointment, I would need to take it. It would be pointless or even seem rude to argue the date; just take it, so ultimately, something else would have to move, and that creates an avalanche of changes.

But hey! It's her, it's her predicament. Whatever she gives you, take it, and make it fit in your schedule somehow, even though on the 12 weeks, everything feels so set.

So, I finally got an appointment from her after chasing her Personal Assistant countless times. It was on a

Tuesday and I had to, of course, change things around, but I was relieved it was in the diary. I was so keen to meet with her that even though the appointment was at 1pm, I was in a coffee shop at 9am going through my presentation and various bits, preparing myself for the 100th time. I was nervous. This was a normal meeting for her, but for me, it was important to make a good impression. After all, the more I could get in terms of orders, the better it was for my target and making an impression on my boss. Everything was quite square within this company, and there was little room for error. They prepped it all for you, but if you could gain more from this meeting, you were seen as the one being of a commercial mind. So, basically, this meeting was an important one.

I put on my suit, red lipstick, and ensured I wore the 15 items of makeup requested by this company. Even though I was nervous, I was as ready as I could be, and I was eager to meet this important buyer that everyone knew. I wanted to be on her radar, and my name was going to be going places. That's how it felt.

Around 11am, I got a phone call. The manager of a counter about 1.5 hours away from London called me, panicking and in a state of shock. I asked what was the matter, and she proceeded to tell me that one of her girls got caught stealing. The security manager had suspected her for some time and found a substantial amount of products in her locker. They were now taking her home with the police to check her room. She had an unopened shirt stuck in her trousers, and that's how they caught her. The worst thing about all of this was that she was far from being a Flossy. She became one in that one phone call, but no one would have suspected anything. So the shock was real for all of us. The manager was crying, and the department manager was also in shock. I needed to go and support as the police needed me to sign some paperwork and deal with the unpleasant things that this type of situation demands.

Now I was feeling super stressed. I was really feeling the pressure, and on top of it all, I was thinking of my planner and the fact that none of it could handle any last-minute changes as it was all so set. I called my boss, and she told me that I had to go over there and deal with it. She could hear in my voice that I was panicking too as I asked her, "But I am meant to meet the buyer at 1pm. I really don't know when I am going to be able to fit her in. Should I stay and meet with her and then go?"

"Valerie, this is an emergency, especially since the police are involved. If you have the appointment that will last one hour, you will finish at 2pm, and by the time you go home, get your car, and drive there, you will deal with everything by 5 or 6pm with the traffic. If you go now, you will arrive by at least 1 to 2pm. It's much better at this stage to go now. I will call the buyer and reschedule."

In my head, I thought, "If it was that easy to get an appointment with this buyer since she has her direct phone number, why did she let me struggle so much with arranging all of this in the first place!"

I begrudgingly left the coffee shop to get my car at home. I refuse to even write what I was shouting in the car, as this book will avoid that type of profanity. But I was ready to give Flossy a piece of my mind when I got there. I was so upset and annoyed that this was happening when it was my chance to shine with the buyer. How dare she do all of that stealing? It's so selfish of her. Most of all, I was starting to feel really stressed out, and my chest was feeling so tight that I found it hard to breathe at the thought of changing an appointment with this difficult buyer. My Journey Planner had little room to move anything around, and everything felt so tight. But I was powering through and drove to deal with the situation.

This type of situation is never nice. It's the part of leadership that no one wants to deal with, but as your title is manager, you have to. I quickly realized that my selfish thoughts were nothing compared to what was happening here. It was all very sad and rather disturbing. I calmed things down while carrying on building the relationship with the department manager. After all, she still needs to trust that we are all working together to overcome what was happening.

I came home that night feeling sad and tired, but also still really stressed about my journey planner. When can I see the buyer? This is one of my biggest accounts, and it's a Christmas order. It's July, and all orders for Christmas have to be finalized by the end of July. It's a given in the industry, hence why we talk about Christmas in July.

Along with the sadness comes anxiety. I am not sure I can cope with the amount of work to be done, let alone looking after my two young girls and changing my diary around for a diva buyer. I call my boss to give her feedback. She can hear I am stressed and asks me. I refuse to tell her, as after all, I am "Valerie who can handle anything!" But I am also French and young, and the stress oozes out of me.

She tells me we need to meet, let's do that tomorrow at a hotel that is near for both of us (well, near is 1.5 hours away, but that's the kind of traveling you had to do!). I then say, "But I have no space to move my appointments tomorrow, so how can I focus on everything, etc.?" She insists. She is my boss. I have to go. Now I am really super stressed and cry over my Journey planner."

We meet the following day and that's where she really teaches me about time management and the system I am about to show you is what she told me over 25 years ago, I still do it, I did tweak it and changed a few things but the core of it remains the same. After all, you will find that I don't really care if you use the latest app or software or if you are paper based, it's how you are managing your time that matters.

She then told me two important things I needed to hear:

1. You will never finish your to do list, so if you know that, it's a matter or organising your priorities on a weekly basis.
2. At the time, when you got that phone call, what became important? The buyer or the police arresting Flossy? Well the police I tell her. Was it part of your job to deal with it? Yes. Did that become your priority? Yes. So on the day, did you do your job? Yes. Something can become a priority and being flexible on how you deal with it is important, but most of all, if you have zero system to fall

back on, you will then become overwhelmed and actually feel that you have zero control over your time

As she was talking to me, I realized there was also one main ingredient to time management that has stuck with me throughout my career: you make a priority what you believe is a priority.

If I said to you right now, "I am going to take you on holiday in a couple of weeks, sending you a couple of thousand pounds in your bank account, and just all I ask is for you to find the flights and the hotel," you would suddenly find the time to look for our well-deserved break without a second thought over your to-do list.

To me, time management is simply a way to organize ourselves and feel on top of everything we are dealing with. And if you really want to achieve something, you will, because you have the power to achieve whatever you have set out to do. Look at where you are now! It's never by accident.

Yes, a lot of business owners I have met felt the need to open something and never learned the financial side of things, learning as they go along. But ultimately, they have succeeded in achieving something. Now, with the structure and time management at the forefront of everything, they will be able to surpass whatever they even thought was impossible.

―――

12 Time Management Principles

1. PLEDGE

A lot of times, working with managers, I realized that very few do what they say they will do because of time, which is where frustration mounts for everyone working with them. As I rose in the ranks of my roles, I wanted to be different and ensure that I made my team feel the way I wanted to feel when I was myself working under a boss. Treat them how you want to be treated. I want them to feel heard, but most of all, I want them to feel that they are working in an efficient and driven organization. I believe that if you are focused, even laser-sharp focused on your goals, you will be surprised how fast you achieve them and even surpass yourself with a team that is fully on board.

So writing a pledge is important at this stage, especially for time management as it is so difficult to stick to that routine. It will allow you to have a contract with yourself and make a serious promise that you will work on it.

I would like you to write a pledge. A promise to yourself that you are going to be fully committed to Time Management. Here is mine:

> I pledge that I will commit to Time Management in order to create the best results for myself and those around me. I will follow my weekly routine and ensure that I will always be honest and reasonable with myself when it comes to my time. Since I want a work-life balance and I know that my Time Management will make me achieve my goal, I am fully committed to making it happen. To build my dream, I understand that Time Management is the key to feeling good about my work and empowering everyone around me by being efficient, focused, and handling many projects. I love my system in place, I believe in myself, I trust that I can do this by making time for time management.

Now take time to write down your own pledge. It's important that you use your own words, something that you will adhere to and believe in. Add it as your screensaver, on top of your office computer, gold paint it, whatever it takes, make that commitment and revisit it daily if necessary, especially at the beginning of your journey with Time Management. Mine is in my diary, at full view if I need it, it was in my office next to my vision for everyone to see beforehand.

2. VISUALISE

Now ask yourself, "Why do I need more time?"

Visualise whatever it is that you want to achieve/create. Is it to play piano? Have a Spa day? Discipline that troublesome staff member? Start up another business? Do more training for my team? Learn to scuba dive? Even if it's to simply go on holiday feel it, be it and be part of it. Visualisation will focus you on whatever it is you want to achieve. Visualisation enables you to have a day off without feeling guilty because you are on top of things and you have been visualising yourself achieving that goal. It's so important to see you there, achieving that goal and the way to structure yourself is by creating your work-life balance and feel good about it all. By eradicating your guilt and visualising your dream, you are one step closer to achieving it.

3. TIDY

A tidy home is a tidy mind, as simple as that. In order to fully focus, your surroundings need to be completely decluttered. I'm not saying you need to redecorate your house or office, but take a moment to assess how much more streamlined your working environment could be. Set aside a day, a week, or even a month to tidy up and clear out any unnecessary paperwork. Do you really need it? Is it valuable? One of the biggest reasons for holding onto clutter is the feeling of 'just in case I need it' or the thought that 'I must have kept that for a reason'. To address this, designate one drawer for items that you are unsure about. Personally, I took photos of all the items I had kept for years and years, and saved them in a folder online. It's amazing how much lighter you feel after decluttering. So before you even dive into time management strategies, I invite you to have a good old-fashioned clear-out and tidy-up. Be ruthless - anything over two years old that you haven't used since is likely to stay that way for a long time. Come back when you've done it - you'll feel so satisfied and your mind will be decluttered. This is not a groundbreaking concept, but it's an effective habit that can sometimes get overlooked.

Declutter now!

4. UNDERSTAND

You will never, ever, finish your to do list. Once you have accepted that, it's simply a matter of organisation. By understanding that you will always have something to do, you will then just create a habit and this becomes a pattern in the way you organise yourself.

5. THE POWER OF ONE

Now here some must haves:

→ One diary

→ One to do list

Diaries everywhere? Lists on your phone? In your post it notes (these should be banned from everywhere!)? On your computer? STOP!! Enough is enough!

Indulge yourself with the purchase of one new diary but stop the complication of too many tools, too many written papers or phone lists. The power of ONE is the key to remain focused on the given tasks and it's amazing how it keeps your mind focused and less scattered. Now choose which it will be and stick to that.

6. TOOLS

My To Do list is quite simple. It consists of one column with BUSINESS tasks and a DONE column which I tick as I go along. However, it's important to have your personal To Do list on there as well. If you have a personal list somewhere else, chances are you won't look at it and will panic when you do because there's some crucial job you had completely forgotten about. Combining the two together is a winner. It's so simple and avoids complications.

	WORK	DONE	PERSONAL	DONE
1				
2				
3				
4				
5				
6				
7				
8				
9				
10				
11				
12				
13				
14				
15				
16				
17				
18				
19				
20				

Now, I know you might want something a lot more fancy, like the latest app that would appeal to you more than this! Rest assured, I'm okay with it. You can use any application that takes your fancy, but you must stick to one tool. The minute you have one of the mentioned, plus a phone list, plus a notebook, plus a book for training, plus a book for advanced training, etc. is the minute you will run back into old habits that clutter your mind and systems. Keep it to one system and one way of dealing with it. In essence, the tool you are using is fine by me. Over the years, I was introduced to these apps, but I continue with my system as everything is under one spreadsheet. Simple and effective is the key. Do what talks to you the most. Now, having a book for training is good, as long as you extract the things to do and add them to your list rather than use it for another to-do list. Become strict with your habit and regimented; otherwise, your bad habits will come back in a flash.

7. IT'S ALL IN THE DETAIL

Once you have the To Do list, your mind is tidy, your surroundings decluttered, take a look at your tasks and differentiate between the bigger tasks and the smaller ones.

Having decided which are the bigger tasks, write down as much detail with regard to these as possible map them out. For example, when I wanted to write this book, I didn't just put: 'Write book on micromanagement' on my To Do list as it would be too generic; I put the date I wanted to finish it by and dissected all of the subjects around writing a book:

→ The marketing around it: branding, social media, email marketing, videos

→ Finding a publisher (even that was drilled down to self publishing, hybrid publishing, publisher specialising in such books etc.)

→ The PR companies, contacts of influencers, industry specific events

→ The cost and budget around it

→ The titles

→ The references

→ Contacts to support my research

Basically, everything short of actually writing the book. This way your To Do list will be far less daunting and your brain can process the small tasks more easily. If I had written 'Write book on micromanagement' I would have spent far too much time procrastinating as a consequence of feeling overwhelmed by the task ahead.

I remember one of my friend inadvertently saw my to-do list on the side of my desk and just laughed! "Omg Valerie! You have on there buy knickers for your daughters?! Why??? Can't you remember that?!"

Valid point and we had a laugh about it but the fact is that by having it on my to-do list, I am able to stop thinking about it and act upon when I can go and buy them whilst prioritising them on one of my visit to a client near the shop. My daughters will never be knickerless and I can stop thinking about it as it's going to be dealt with when dealing with my weekly To-do list. Have you ever suddenly thought: "oh I must do that" whilst in a shower or popping up in some other random place suddenly? Well by writing all of these small details it avoids that as your freeing your brain from these tasks, they are taken care of.

8. ONCE A WEEK

Now, here is the non-negotiable aspect of Time Management. Once a week, on the same day, same time, you will sit down and create a comprehensive, thorough To-Do list. There are no excuses. This must become your routine, your new habit, and it never stops unless you are on holiday. It's okay if it's every Friday morning or Saturday morning or even Monday evenings. But it's the same day and ideally the same time. Just put it in your diary for the year ahead.

In order for Time Management to work, you need to make time for time management. I revisit my To-Do list every Monday morning. I set two hours from nine to eleven. Over the years, the day has changed but my Monday admin, since being a consultant, has allowed me to feel recentered and reset for the weekend and the week ahead.

The way I implement my To-Do list is by having it saved online, and every week, I cut and paste it on a new tab, add the date on the tab, delete everything I have done, and add everything else I need to add from the week I just had. By keeping a weekly tab of my To-Do list, it allows me to realize all of the small steps I have made, and we all know what that does: it mounts up to a giant step by the end of the year. Celebrating the achievements, as small as they are, is so important.

It should look like this:

25th of May	1st of June	8th of June	15th of June	22nd of June	29th of June

I then print it and use that printout for the week. Part of me loves writing on it as it allows me to feel that I am actively using it rather than just looking at it periodically if it were to stay on my computer. Plus, I want to avoid using my laptop all the time, so having it at hand allows me to write everything that is coming up that week. Then the following week, it gets added to the computer list, and the routine is set, as I do this weekly regardless, unless on holidays.

9. PRIORITISE YOUR PRIORITIES

Everyone that I have managed through leadership programs seems to struggle with this one the most. We make the mistake of making everything a priority, causing us to either give up or procrastinate. Get your diary and assess when your tasks need to be done by. What can wait? What is urgent? And if you have five tasks for tomorrow, which of these can really wait for another day? It is a matter of managing expectations. You should always think of your top ten priorities for the week. Everything else on your to-do list can wait.

The fact is that we have a tendency to think everything is a priority, and that can cause stress or anxiety, but in reality, things can wait or be added as a priority the following week. For example, if my accountant is asking me something and the deadline is Friday, I know that he will stop work on the Friday afternoon, so if I have a busy week, I can add it as a priority on Monday and deal with it first thing Monday morning. It gives me more time and generates a strong sense of achievement.

If you really look at your to-do list right now, not everything is a priority; it's just a matter of managing your to-do list. Once I have printed my list, I highlight the ten priorities or twelve, depending on whether I am busy that week. Then, I look at my diary and work out which priority will realistically be done that day. I usually work on two priorities a day, whether they are professional or personal. I make it work depending on the day ahead. It can be a quick priority, done in between clients, or if it's a lengthy task, in which case I block a couple of hours for that to give me enough time for that particular task.

It is so important to set that time aside for you to understand and analyze your to-do list, as it will allow you to have the headspace to think. On top of that, it will eradicate all of the little details that can become too stressful. If you are creating a to-do list and priority list from Monday to Friday, it will give you five days of being able to achieve your top priorities.

2 priorities a day = 10 priorities a week

This way, your top ten priorities are scattered throughout the week, two at a time, making it more likely for you to achieve them. For example, if you finish your priorities for Monday, avoid doing other priorities and trust your process. Simply revisit your to-do list and work on that. You will find that your work will flow more smoothly, and you will achieve more than you ever thought possible.

I used to have this next to my to-do list and printed it, but it's up to you to choose whatever method helps your mind. Now, I prefer to highlight the priorities as I go through my to-do list and then allocate them per day.

		Monday
	1	Preperation for training in Morocco
	2	Email to Accountant
		Tuesday
	1	Email Follow up for Client A
	2	Call sister for holiday
		Wednesday
	1	No Priority - training day
	2	
		Thursday
	1	Call Association to secure appointment
	2	Prep for video marketing
		Friday
	1	Collect dress in dry cleaner
	2	Book holidays
		Saturday
	1	Gym with Friends
	2	Create a template for Email follow up
		Sunday
	1	Rest day
	2	
		Extra
	1	Secure Graphic designer for book
	2	Revisit client journey for reception programme

It is so important to be truthful when you add your priorities daily, as too often my clients fail because they add too much to their day. Making your priorities or your to-do list unrealistic is only going to reinforce the sense of having to control everything as well as generating a sense of frustration.

The other aspect of failure when it comes to priorities is that we tend to add them daily but maybe on Wednesday, in this instance, we are in training all day so we will be unable to have time for any to-do list! So it's unnecessary to add anything on Wednesday; it's pointless. If you have the time to do something from your to-do list, then great, it's a bonus. But if you were busy all day then that's okay because you hadn't planned it, so in essence, you are on top of everything.

Thinking strategically at this stage is absolutely crucial, be honest with your time, and remember that your priority can be a professional or personal one. Keep it varied so you never get bored, keep it light and focused.

10. DO THE TASK YOU DON'T WANT TO DO FIRST

There is a great book I recommend called 'Eat 'That Frog by Brian Tracy - read it! Brian Tracy advises us to do the big tasks first, the ones you really don't want to do. This will not only give you a huge sense of satisfaction, but it will also make you much more productive. It really works. It's a proven formula.

Every week, I do a task that I am unmotivated by or one that I've been putting off for ages. It feels so good when it's done, and early in the week is even better as everything else feels so easy after that. It keeps the mindset alive, lightens the to-do list, and clears your mind at the same time.

Remember, we tend to prioritize what we believe is a priority and what we want to do; it's so much easier that way. So challenge yourself and do that task that has been in your mind for a while - it feels so much better. I love mornings, so I will always do the 'difficult' tasks in the morning so that they are out of the way, and as early on in the week as possible, as I tend to be more motivated and less distracted by everything else.

11. CREATIVITY

Sometimes people perceive being organized in this way as being rigid, perhaps a little too systematic, as opposed to spontaneous, loose, and free. They therefore mistakenly believe it to be anti-creativity.

What it actually does is give you more time to be creative. In fact, it's a good idea to have something with you at all times on which to write down all your creative ideas. We call this a Brain Dumping Book, although a friend of mine thought a Creativity Book was a lot nicer. Yes, I have to agree on that one! Call it what you wish, this little book of magic allows you to write down whatever you want whenever it occurs to you. This is the opposite of a To-Do list; it's merely somewhere to jot down your thoughts. If you don't want to carry another book around with you, you can use Evernotes, a small notepad, or your phone notes.

Then, on the day of revisiting my To-Do list, I go through this book. There may be some great ideas in there worth exploring, others that need to be crossed out. By writing down these thoughts, it not only allows you to nurture your creativity but also declutter your mind – hence the name Brain Dumping. If you don't have something with you to write down your ideas, it's amazing how quickly you can forget them. I have something next to me as I usually wake up with some kind of inspiration or something I must write down.

12. MINDFULNESS

Once you have decided on which priorities you will be completing on which day, it's important to switch off distractions such as your phone, social media, and email notifications. Multi-tasking is not allowed! As one of my favorite quotes goes, "Multi-tasking is the art of messing several things at once." While persuading people to do this is the biggest challenge I face when teaching time management, you will be surprised at how much you can get done by doing so. Otherwise, there is a great danger you will stray into the hedge of procrastination.

When you are setting time aside for your To-do list, those two precious hours of calm and recentering for the week ahead, take that time for yourself and avoid social media or videos in the background. Use what works for you, whether it's listening to music or another method, but focus solely on the task at hand. Revisiting and fine-tuning your system is also important, even if you are already good at time management. As the saying goes, "You can't teach an old dog new tricks," so it is up to you to commit and create good habits that work for you.

One book that I have found helpful when it comes to organization is 'Getting Things Done' by David Allen.

To recap, The 12 Key Essentials To Time Management:

1. Write Down Your Pledge
2. Visualise Why You Want More Time
3. Tidy Your Space
4. You Will Never Finish Your To Do List So It's A Matter Of Organising
5. The Power Of One To-Do List: Personal and Professional
6. Chose Your To-Do List Tool
7. It's All In The Detail
8. Once A Week Make Time For Time Management
9. Prioritise 10 Priorities and Allocate Two A Day
10. Do What You Want To Avoid First
11. Use A Dumping Brain/Creativity Book
12. Be Mindful

I should add another one to emphasise my hate relationship with those:

Ban Post-It Notes!

The Time Killers

So, where does it go wrong?

Presenting to you, The Time Killers. The main issue is we useless at managing the time killers. These consist of five elements:

1. PEOPLE

The excuses are endless: the customer who wants to chat, the therapist who is running late, your friend who wants to organize her hen party. Make time for them, but be firm and understand why you need to be firm. For example, one lady who would come for a manicure every week always wanted to talk to me. I would oblige because she was a great customer, but I used to mix my meetings with her. One week I would give her my undivided attention, and another I would just give her five minutes. The key is that I would make it clear from the start, "How are you, Lady Roskall? I have five minutes for you, then need to go on a call. Tell me…" Setting your expectations is so important to your communication.

She would have my undivided attention for those five minutes, ensuring that I would sit at her eye level and smile throughout the countless stories she used to tell me. Another time, a therapist stopped me on my way to the office and said, "I want to talk to you." "Okay," I said, "What is it regarding?" "My holidays," she said. So I kindly told her that I was really busy today, but I will add her to my diary tomorrow and ensure she has 15 minutes blocked out tomorrow in her diary. The following day, I needed to ensure that I would keep to my words and meet with her; otherwise, that's when she could become annoyed or demotivated. I do what I say I will do.

Now, if you had looked into my diary, you would have realized that I could have seen her on the day she wanted to see me. But I am in charge of my time, and it's important that the team has undivided attention, but that has to be in my own time. Otherwise, I feel swallowed by everyone else's stuff but mine. Being in charge of your time has to become a priority. Balancing your needs and those of others is an art, and to me, where you can be seen as the leader that has it all under some control.

The point is this: You are in charge of your time. You know when you can take time for the people around you. And that phone? It is off until you finish your task. If you're worried about urgent matters, then look at your phone every hour if you need. You can even set an alarm to remind you so you never have to keep checking. Chances are most things can wait.

In this particular spa, we had an open-door policy as it was a very American culture. I loved it but knew it would jeopardize my focus. Like anything I love, I compromise and ensure that there is still a way for all of us to work together on this. I mean, being disrupted because someone comes to the office and asks questions such as what uniform size should I order? Or where are the gloves? Or the story of their customers because there is so much energy when you work with customers so closely, it's good for them to be able to offload. But you, on the other hand, have to keep it together and smile through adversity. Although that's a big word when it comes to people disturbing your peace and quiet, that time you have set aside to do something so important. Nonetheless, I know that it can be so disruptive and difficult to handle those disturbances because we love people and want to be there. We also want them to know we are there for anything. And because somewhere along the lines, perhaps, we are procrastinating with other conversations because maybe the priorities of today are simply annoying.

Any way it comes, it's important that you take control of your time. It's yours and yours alone, so it's up to you to manage it. The bottom line is that you can focus on your time to ensure that you are managing it to your advantage.

I had a meeting with everyone and said:

Okay, so I love the open door policy, but we are going to have to add some rules to it. The door will be wide open until 2pm in the afternoon, as I estimated that would be enough time for the morning to afternoon shift to have support. I never want to be disturbed unless there is an emergency. I estimate that an emergency consists of; fire, it would be nice for you all to let me know if there is a fire somewhere; death, I would also want to know in the unlikely event of that happening; blood, but I don't want just a little bit of blood, I want a big splash of blood (humor here, obviously there are processes for this difficult and rare event!) Unless those scenarios are happening, you must never enter at your own leisure. It must always be before 2pm."

From two to five, I estimated that it gave me enough time for crucial reports, networking, meetings, or any kind of work that I needed to focus on. It allowed me to be efficient and focused for the day. It's important for you to assess how you function and revisit how you can manage that.

The tone was set, I was never bothered in the afternoon and was able to be so much more focused and efficient in my role. Now, I really want to emphasize the fact that time management is your assessment and you must revisit what suits you.

2. NEVER TAKING TIME TO REASSESS OUR TO-DO LIST

If you never take time for time management regularly, you will become overwhelmed. Or even if you do your To-Do list but manage it sporadically, you will find that you never feel on top of things and constantly worry. The key to time management, as mentioned above, is getting into new habits. Your priority should be attending to your To-Do list on a weekly basis. Tick off the jobs you have completed throughout the week - there is no need to keep revising, just work on adding what comes up and ticking what you have managed to achieve on that day. It's fascinating how the To-Do list can work against us, but a lot of the time, when we do a time management program, this is what I see:

→ Too many unrealistic tasks set under one day which sets you up for failure and that's when you have a tendency to give up.

→ Very generic headings that are too broad, and therefore the stress is far from being relieved from everything that needs to be done, as mentioned before under one heading can be at least 10 various things to do. Ensure you dissect your task to the minute details.

→ Hardly anything on the To-Do list which makes me wonder if the job itself is structured properly.

→ On the other side, micromanagers tend to have a to-do list of 80 things to do and never see the benefits of delegation, so the list can become very overwhelming.

→ Little or zero time set aside for time management, which is so ironic but true. If you avoid setting that time aside weekly on the same day, you will never feel completely on top of your work.

→ To-do list achieved very quickly: I am always dubious about this one, as although it's a great achievement, it makes me wonder if everything is looked into and whether the delegation is done correctly. There is something to be said about being efficient, but we have so much to build on when we have our business. How can it be completely finished? I have weeks when my to-do list is lighter so I can schedule more time for myself, but there is always something to do to grow the business. So ask yourself the right question: Is the business where it should be?

. . .

So the key is to start a new structure for yourself to ensure that your planner is up to date and your weekly time aside is set for the year ahead!

I have a yearly planner where I add my weekly Time Management set up, my meetings with my managers, and the monthly required meetings. The minute you understand that your communication and your time are crucial to empowering others and feeling on top of everything to build your business forward, then that is the minute you will make time for your Time Management and never take that off your diary. It simply helps you to recenter, think, process, and reassess.

What is intriguing is that when we had the lockdown, I spoke to so many people who, in some ways, wished it was different than going through a pandemic, but they managed to recenter and reset through that time out. So my question to you now is: what is stopping you from simply taking two hours aside to plan ahead? Especially if it makes you feel great - everyone I speak to feels wonderful with this system! So why stop?!?!

3. BAD HABITS

If you're not careful, your bad habits will come back to haunt you quickly. It takes 66 days to form a habit, but with time management, you really need to commit to it for three solid months. It will then become part of your natural routine. Something magical always happens on the third month: you become efficient, and you like it! The more you like it, the more you will want to stick to it.

Bad habits are there to haunt you, and going back to the default mechanism is so much easier than carrying on. The worst part when I speak about habits to my clients is that there is guilt and frustration oozing out of them when they talk about their bad habits! In any operational business, a business where we turn up and do the same things day in and day out, it's so easy to set up a routine that in some ways disturbs your setup. Boredom can cause so much procrastination.

So it's down to you to be focused enough. If you know something needs to change, if you are on the brink of burnout, if you feel overwhelmed, if you feel you are on that wheel, if you are constantly doing the same things and expecting different results, it's time to revisit your time management and create a strong focus. This is particularly good to do along with a yearly planner and your vision for the year, as it will enable you to focus on your overall goal, and that in itself is so powerful.

What I have seen with bad habits is that, most of the time, there is a lack of direction and far from waking you up in the morning with clear energy and determination, so everything feels like a distant future. So, your strategy becomes one of the most crucial elements of what you must work on, and the first thing I do with my clients. Without that, procrastination overtakes everything.

4. AVOIDING PRIORITIES

When something unexpected becomes a priority for the week, it can be frustrating, but it's important not to beat yourself up about it. This happens all the time, and it's likely due to a lack of processes and foundation to fall back on. If something else takes over for a week, two weeks, or a month, then it has become your priority, and you have achieved your aim. Having a process to fall back on can be your savior. Remember, the to-do list will never be fully achieved, and priorities change from time to time. Accepting this and managing your time accordingly is key.

Feeling overwhelmed with the number of priorities to manage can also be a challenge. It's essential to understand that not everything is a priority, and if something is a priority, block out a few days in your schedule to get on top of it all. Alternatively, it may be time to invest in a PA or a virtual assistant. Often, a lack of understanding of priorities comes down to a lack of planning, not knowing when a task needs to be done, and realistically, some tasks deemed as important can wait a week or so.

5. PROCRASTINATION

Oh, my favorite one! I am fascinated by procrastination and why we procrastinate. Everything I mentioned above is true to encourage procrastination but it also is a deep habit rooted inside of any procrastinators.

To understand what causes procrastination (outside of conditions such as attention-deficit/hyperactivity disorder, where executive functioning issues might interfere with task completion), it's important to be clear about what it is — and isn't. Procrastination is different from delaying a task because you need to talk to someone who isn't available, or not getting around to reading a literary classic such as 'Moby Dick.' Fuschia Sirois, a professor of psychology at the University of Sheffield in England, defines procrastination this way: "The voluntary, unnecessary delay of an important task, despite knowing you'll be worse off for doing so."

Sacrificing sleep to make time for yourself? Tips to stop 'revenge bedtime procrastination.'

On its surface, procrastination is an irrational behavior, Sirois said, "Why would somebody put something off to the last minute, and then they're stressed out of their mind, and they end up doing a poor job or less than optimal job on it? And then they feel bad about it afterward, and it may even have implications for other people."

The reason, she said, has to do with emotional self-regulation — and, in particular, an inability to manage negative moods around a certain task. We usually don't procrastinate on fun things, she said. We procrastinate on tasks we find "difficult, unpleasant, aversive or just plain boring or stressful." If a task feels especially overwhelming or provokes significant anxiety, it's often easiest to avoid it.

Another reason people procrastinate, Sirois said, is because of low self-esteem. One might think, "I'm never going to do this right," or, "What will my boss think if I screw up?"

Ferrari theorizes that there are three types of procrastinators: thrill-seekers, who crave the rush of putting off tasks until the last minute and believe they work best under pressure; avoiders, who procrastinate to avoid being judged for how they perform; and indecisives, who have difficulty making important or stressful decisions, often because they're ruminating over several choices.

→ DANGERS OF PROCRASTINATION

It is important to note that procrastination can have serious consequences not just in terms of productivity but also in terms of mental and physical health. Chronic procrastinators are at higher risk of stress-related health problems and are more likely to experience symptoms of depression and anxiety. They may also delay preventive healthcare, which can lead to more serious health issues down the road.

In addition to mental health problems, procrastination can also affect sleep patterns and increase the risk of heart problems. Research has shown that procrastinators are more likely to experience sleep problems and engage in "revenge bedtime procrastination," which can lead to shorter sleep duration and daytime sleepiness. Furthermore, a study led by Fuschia Sirois (Journal of Behavioural Medicine, 2015) found that people with heart disease were more likely to identify as procrastinators and were less likely to take action to manage their illness.

In short, procrastination can have serious consequences on both mental and physical health. It is important to recognize and address procrastination habits in order to prevent these negative outcomes.

→ OVERCOMING PROCRASTINATION

By overcoming your tendency to stall, you can improve your mental and physical well-being. Here are some expert suggestions.

Practice self-compassion. Procrastinators are often hard on themselves. They might feel guilty about letting others down or be appalled by their own slowness. Sirois's research indicates a connection between procrastination and low levels of self-compassion. To counter that, treat yourself with kindness and understanding. "Just sort of recognizing that, yeah, maybe I screwed up and maybe I could have gotten started earlier, but I don't need to beat myself up," she said. Tell yourself: "I'm not the first person to procrastinate, and I won't be the last." Sirois notes that self-compassion doesn't make people lazy.

On the contrary, "research has shown that it actually increases people's motivation to improve themselves," she said.

Ferrari offers a similar suggestion to avoiders, who procrastinate for fear of being judged: focus on doing your best, instead of getting caught in the trap of worrying about what others think.

Attach meaning to the task. One of the best ways to stop procrastinating, Sirois said, is to find meaning in the task in question. Write down why it's important to you: It could be because getting it done on time is helpful to other people or because it will help you avoid negative repercussions, such as a late fee or bad grade. Think about how completing it will be valuable to your personal growth or happiness. Doing so will help you feel more connected to the task and less likely to procrastinate, Sirois said.

Start small. Ferrari likes to reference the expression, "Cannot see the forest for the trees." The problem of procrastinators is the opposite: All they can see is the forest. And they become so overwhelmed by the size of the forest (or project) that they're paralyzed into inactivity. "I tell them to cut down one tree at a time," he said. "You can't do one tree? Give me three branches." Once you've gotten started and made even a small bit of progress on your task, there's a good chance you'll keep going, he said. This can be particularly helpful to indecisive procrastinators, or "procs," as Ferrari calls them. These people, who are often perfectionists, do best when they split up a task into manageable parts, rather than feeling pressure to perform perfectly on a big, daunting project.

Another tip, he said, is to set deadlines for yourself for those small steps. If you're someone who thrives under pressure, doing so can help replicate the adrenaline rush you get when you wait until the last minute.

Carefully choose which task you do first. Some people want to get the most unpleasant tasks out of the way, while others "psych themselves up by doing smaller things," said Gretchen Rubin, an author whose books include "Better Than Before," which dispenses advice on curbing procrastination. "As they accrue small, easy accomplishments, they feel ready to do that big one." It's a matter of personal preference and knowing yourself. But she added that, when people build up to the most daunting task of the day, they might use other work as a stall tactic.

Situate yourself in a spot that's interruption-free. This is particularly important for demanding tasks, Rubin said. We get interrupted constantly: by our phones, our families, howling dogs, the TV. But once you're interrupted, she said, it's much harder to resume the task you finally started.

Be aware of the "procrasticlearing" trap. Often, procrastinators are struck with the urge to tidy their space before they start working on a task — as in, "Oh, I can't possibly focus until I clean up my office," Rubin said. It's one thing to spend 15 minutes straightening up the immediate area where you're working. "But if I'm like, I need to go through all those shelves back there and alphabetize my books and dust them and maybe paint the bookshelves," she said, you might be "procrasticlearing." One way to know for sure is if the moment the task you were cleaning ahead of is completed, all desire to tidy and organize vanishes. Being mindful of this tendency can help prevent it from inhaling half your day.

Reward yourself. Many teachers and parents use the Premack principle, which essentially stipulates that "something somebody wants to do becomes the reward for something they don't want to do," Ferrari said. If you have 12 dirty dishes in your sink and your favorite TV show comes on in half an hour, make a deal with yourself: You can only watch it if you do the dishes first. The idea can be applied to almost anything that you're pushing off, he said.

Speaking of rewards: Ferrari also believes a change in societal attitude could help. Our society doesn't reward the early bird, he notes. People who pay bills or taxes late are punished with fines, for example, but there's no reward for those who submit them early. Consistently rewarding earliness, he said, could help curb procrastination.

Enlist external help. Decades ago, professors would put a note about their projects on their office doors, and students could come by and hold them accountable, Ferrari said. It was called "public posting." There's an easy way to continue this tradition: social media. Post about your goals on Facebook or Twitter, and ask your network to hold you accountable. If you want to go to a big concert, for example, "tell your friends, 'I will not buy a ticket to Lizzo unless I do A, B, and C, and you've got to hold me accountable,'" Ferrari suggested. "Don't let me slide by on this."

It is important for me to share with you the references and understanding of why procrastination can take over your focus and work. Our clients often seek one-on-one coaching to make themselves accountable, and procrastination disappears when we provide clear steps through small achievements. Anyone who claims they can change your business in 30 days is selling an unrealistic dream. Any business that deals with customers requires careful planning and attention to detail, which can be accomplished little by little. A few tweaks can make a difference in your business, so let time management be the start of it all. As for our Marc and Marie's out there, it's simple: the more you let go, the more you can achieve. One of my clients said to me, "If I told you I was thinking of having another day away from the business a year ago, I would have had a panic attack! Now I can see how it works, and we are achieving the same revenue with less costs as everything is streamlined without her cutting hair and juggling all those plates."

"I know," I said, "it's all about understanding why time management is your friend and how structure can make it work."

My Time Management Update

Having worked with my business partner Amy Gordon for over two years now (she joined me in July 2020, in the midst of the pandemic), it has been really interesting to see how she manages her time. As mentioned before, I always believe that when you keep learning about a subject, even if you are good at it, you should always assess if it needs tweaking or if it's in good shape, as it will reinforce that what you are doing is still valid and strong. It's crucial that you revisit your Time Management process, particularly when you are feeling overwhelmed. Amy has run a successful clinic in the UK and is a crucial part of The Delforge Group© by coaching owners and managers alike to grow in their roles and develop their soft skills.

We have been working ultra-hard during the pandemic to empower as many people as possible, and my diary went from busy to ultra-busy. I had never realized that, even though my Time Management is on point, I was getting rather overwhelmed with the amount of work we needed to deliver. Plus, I was traveling to my clients before the pandemic. Suddenly, my home becomes my haven and workplace. Even though it's appealing to work from home, you need to be even more focused on your time management, as your bedroom suddenly can become your office at 6 am in the morning. So even though I powered through and carried on with my system, I felt that I was far from being aligned with it at that stage.

I had to become ultra-strict with myself and encourage my members to have their admin day from home but be very defined in their time management; otherwise, you work at any time, anywhere (kitchen table with everyone running around you) or you are unable to even have a break from your laptop... Unhealthy indeed for both the mind and the body. Amy has been asking me for my holiday dates. "Yeah yeah, I will send them to you," I said. She persisted, but the more she did, the more panicky I was getting. I was just unable to see when I was going to be allowing myself to get away with all of my members and projects that were coming through.

We had a strategy meeting, and she had a look at my diary on my online calendar, which is great as it's online, so my admin team can access it, but it was a sea of blue color. Lunch was nonexistent, and admin time kept being moved around. Me! The Queen of Time Management!

All she did was this:

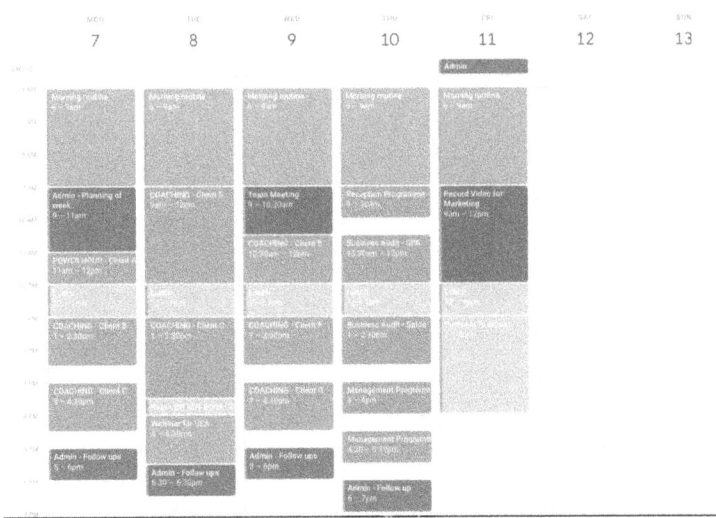

She colour coded my diary which is ultra easy on my online calendar:

→ Lunches and personal stuff in yellow

→ Admin on Monday morning for my to-do list and Friday afternoon for personal bits to do in green

→ Our catch up or any one of the team's in purple

→ Talks and networking in a burgundy colour

→ All of my clients in the normal blue I was used to

The beauty of it is that you can repeat it weekly at the touch of a button and sync it from your phone to your laptop. I left our meeting feeling lighter and refocused. Nothing was done for the workload itself, but knowing that my lunch was set and my admin is now regular for my personal stuff, it means my weekends are never spent playing catch-up. As you grow and handle more, it's key to revisit your time management system, as it matters so much and has a ripple effect on everything you do. Amy also blocks out two hours at a time in her diary for her priorities. If she finishes earlier, she then carries on with her to-do list.

Moral of the story: You can become overwhelmed without even noticing. It's crucial to reassess your workload and check whether it's still working for you. Be honest with your feelings and assess what needs to be done. Those two hours set aside for your time management become a time to set up but also a time to reassess: what can I delegate, what can be done when, and am I still feeling happy with the outcomes? You can be the Queen of Time Management, but it doesn't mean you can't get overwhelmed.

Confession Time!

Marc was so busy with his four salons, and everything being paper-based, he was struggling on a day-to-day basis. He was very much firefighting all of his tasks as they came along without having much of a plan for the long term.

One day, he woke up with an emergency to deal with as a customer was unhappy with the finish of their hair colour she had the day before with another staff member. Not wanting a bad review and ensuring that all clients are happy is paramount to his business, so he had to make the time to invite her again for a colour correction. Having a senior team fully booked, he was the only one that had the capability of doing such a service. Halfway through the correction, he realized he had another appointment, but since he forgot his paper diary, he was unable to contact the person in question and had to send one of his juniors to his home to recoup the diary. He then had to apologize and reschedule the appointment, which in itself generated a knock-on effect to his week. What a stressful situation for Marc but also for everyone involved!

Marc was frustrated as he had so much to do that day, so he ended up finishing at 12 am after a long day of juggling and having to worry about what's next, which is far from being proactive and all systems were going against him. The first thing we did was ensure that his diary was online for reception to see. Whether it's clients or meetings with suppliers, everything is on there, including contact details so his diary management becomes streamlined.

The more organized he is, the more he can handle and create a work-life balance he needs to recenter and refocus.

→ COMMUNICATION

Communication is such an important soft skill and aspect of your role that it becomes essential to revisit how you communicate, from the customer point of view with your marketing to how you empower your team. When it comes to management, there are two important communications:

1. YOUR SELF TALK

The most important communication of all is how you speak to yourself. It is possibly the most impactful when it comes to mindset, but also how you are perceived as a leader. Your self-talk becomes the key to nurturing and keeping your mindset strong. We have a tendency to be very hard on ourselves, and self-talk can become more damaging than ever. As I always say, "To empower others, you must empower yourself first."

I am sure you have seen Dr. Masaru Emoto's experiment and many others conducted online.[1] The results showed that the rice (or apple/strawberry/plant) that heard lovely loving words was still in good condition after a few days/weeks, while the "hate" rice was going moldy and bad. The rice that was ignored did not do so well either.

I have taught my daughters this at an early age as I knew that my self-talk had to be worked on very early on in my career. My grandmothers were incredibly tough ladies, managing farms during the war and had a no-nonsense attitude. My mother had the same ethos and high standards, so I guess, even subconsciously, we have always been very hard on ourselves. Disappointment can be hurtful, perfection can take over, and never being satisfied is also part of it. So what happens then? We can become micromanagers as when we lose a sense of control of something or are not truly satisfied with the outcome, "I'd rather do it myself" comes quickly in our behavior or mind.

So let's be kind to ourselves, but it's easier said than done, and most times it can be so damaging that we are not even aware of it. I realized a while back that my harshness towards myself was going against me. I had just separated and became a single mom, had a management role that was not only demanding but also consuming, as now I had the pressure of relying purely on myself. It becomes extremely damaging to your mindset if you are not careful.

I listened to a podcast (I always regret forgetting to write down the name of it, but forgive me as it was a very long time ago!). This lady mentioned that according to the National Science Foundation, an average person has about 12,000 to 60,000 thoughts per day, although a new study is saying 6,000, so do not quote me on this number. But what was really intriguing is that of those, 80% are negative, and 95% are repetitive thoughts.[2] So it immediately made me think of that rice experiment. If you are talking to yourself in a negative manner and it's on repeat, what is it actually doing to yourself? On top of this, according to an article in Scientific American, "The vast majority of our thinking efforts go on subconsciously. Only one or two of these thoughts are likely to breach into consciousness at a time. Slips of the tongue and accidental actions offer glimpses of our unfiltered subconscious mental life."

As mentioned, we can write a book on this as it's so fascinating, but by all means, it has never been my expertise. However, this lady on the podcast made me realize that I was so hard on myself, and perhaps it was more damaging than I anticipated. She suggested taking a little notepad and pen, keeping them handy at all times so when you remember a thought, you write it down. You do this for three weeks. No matter what thought, just write it down.

Well, that was something else. Not only would I never say these things to my worst enemy, but I was taken aback by the number of thoughts that were so damaging to my mindset: "you're fat, look at your stomach, no one wants you, omg look at these wrinkles, you're always hungry, nothing you can do with these legs, no one likes you, you're too difficult, they talk behind your back, no wonder you can't find a man look at you, you're not the leader they like, you're rubbish, well, that was awful, no one listened, no one cares, you are always alone, everyone is against you, no one likes you..." I mean, come on! None of it was true! How can I lead a team if that's what I think? How can I lead myself, never mind a team, if I don't believe in myself and I put myself down on any occasion that I can? This becomes utterly, incredibly damaging, and the worst part is that it's absolutely, undeniably what I think of myself. I had become the rice that no one loved (well, that's what I thought), including me.

The opposite is strangely the same. Thinking you are it, having an ego the size of a house and never feeling that it's you at any point, so you are not taking the responsibility, as it's never you, it's them, becomes extremely damaging for anyone working for such leaders.

A true leader will always assess and reassess the way they have dealt with situations and revisit the process and create a strong path for success.

A leader that leads with an ego can be hugely successful, but unless they tame it, they can equally be as damaging to their business and the people around them. It is why it is so crucial to assess and reassess your self-talk but also your communication path.

There are so many ways to revisit your self talk. Perhaps the big ego is a little trickier as you have to realise it in the first place, but this is what I do to recenter and revisit my self talks:

→ Meditation is simply the best. It helps in helping you relax and cultivate positive and beneficial thoughts for your mindset. There are plenty of meditation techniques available, but you should explore and practice the ones that resonate with you. I have a friend, Elizabeth Caroline, who studied meditation with a Zen master and now offers mindfulness programs. I love listening to various meditations on YouTube, and I make sure to take at least 30 minutes every morning to meditate and center myself. There is a famous Zen quote that I adore, "You should sit in meditation for twenty minutes every day, unless you're too busy; then you should sit for an hour."

➔ Learned about NLP (Neuro-Linguistic Programming) which is a method of processing thoughts. Instead of thinking, "Oh no, what an awful day. It's raining. I'm fed up," you program your mind to think, "Oh, it's raining. I'm going to take an umbrella." NLP is a widely used and popular program from the 1970s that helps change someone's thoughts and behaviors to achieve desired outcomes.

➔ I counteracted every thought that was negative and that I remembered with a less damaging one.

➔ I started taking care of myself physically by practicing yoga, although I wouldn't consider myself a true yogi since I enjoy changing up my physical activities. Currently, I am looking for a more active lifestyle, so I have hired a personal trainer to help me on a weekly basis. I think there is a lot of pressure to fit into a certain mold, but it's important to remember that you can do what you enjoy, whether that means being a vegan, yoga enthusiast or something else entirely. Don't put too much pressure on yourself, but do make sure to take care of yourself because no one else will do it for you.

→ I started believing in what I could achieve and began taking time to acknowledge my accomplishments each week. I asked myself questions like, "What did I do right this week?" and, "When was the last time I was proud of my achievements?" Instead of focusing on what I didn't do or what I should have done, I started to look at areas for improvement and thought about how I could approach those situations differently in the future. This mindset shift helped me to avoid negative self-talk and celebrate my wins, which I believe is crucial for anyone who wants to be a successful leader.

→ I started to understand that criticism can be really constructive rather than damaging and allows you to refine your leadership.

→ I started to relax in my role and understood that although I have high standards, sometimes we are going to make mistakes as we are dealing with people. We are bound to have misunderstandings and miscommunications sometimes, but it's how we recover from them that is crucial. Customers or staff, for that matter, will always appreciate it if we take responsibility for our mistakes, learn from them and take steps to prevent them from happening again. It's important to have a growth mindset and be open to learning from our mistakes rather than beating ourselves up about them.

→ I created a morning and evening routine that puts me in a great mindset. Again, stop the pressure and do what you feel is right for you, but take that time. And if I go out that day/evening, then it's okay to miss out. Stop feeling guilty, as it gets you nowhere.

→ I listen to podcasts and read books of people that inspire me.

→ I stop being critical about everything and anything just for the sake of it and tame my mind to think more strategically and leave behind what doesn't serve me.

→ I started studying about communication and found it so fascinating I wanted to create workshops around it.

→ I started to know what I enjoyed and what made me miserable so focused my energy on better things.

→ I take two days away from it all in a month to recenter and refocus and sometimes just to do nothing.

Enjoying my own company has been a learning curve that has been so fulfilling and allows me to like myself.

Basically, nurturing yourself is crucial for your authentic leadership to grow. No one can like you if you don't like yourself first. Do you have children? Negotiate that time with your partner. It's so crucial to take a step back, reassess, recenter, and rejuvenate. Otherwise, you are less likely to grow your leadership.

Confession Time!

One day, a staff member of Marie's asked to review their hours, and then another staff member followed suit, with another demanding a weekend off each month due to their long tenure. Marie was taken aback and couldn't understand why they suddenly became so demanding and ungrateful for everything she did for them. She believed that she gave them everything they needed and that they should be happy with their pay, or else they could go work somewhere else and see how they were treated.

My main questions to Marie were: Can you afford to lose them? Can you recruit easily? If the answers are yes, then you can go for what you believe. But I guaranteed her that she would feel the same about the new team whenever she had to recruit again. We looked at the planner, revisited some of the trading hours, checked when we needed each team member, and discussed a plan of action that would be a good outcome for both the employees and the business. I knew that this was against Marie's thought process, and she had to make concessions in her way of thinking. She had to be flexible enough to find a solution that worked for everyone, even though they wanted to reduce their hours. In the end, everyone was happier, and the numbers never suffered.

Marie eventually managed to recruit one more person, and the numbers thrived. Now, instead of thinking only of what she gives, Marie understands that it's a two-way street. Her employees also give a lot through the services they generate. After all, it's impossible to do everything by yourself!

2. YOUR TEAM

When it comes to communication, you need to have this in mind:

➜ TOO MANY MESSAGES KILL THE MESSAGE
➜ TOO LITTLE COMMUNICATION BREEDS FRUSTRATION

Your communication skills will set you up for success as they are at the heart of everything you do. Whether you deal with customers or colleagues, friends or family, it can be difficult to communicate effectively.

However, when we have a lot going on in our personal life or when someone around us is being difficult, it can be even more challenging. We depend a lot on the energy that surrounds us, and sometimes it can cause us to communicate sporadically or even poorly.

Learning how to communicate efficiently and create a smooth working environment should be a priority for you as a leader.

→ MIND YOUR LANGUAGE

In one of my favorite books when it comes to communication, 'Drop the Pink Elephant' by Bill MacFallen, he starts by giving an example of the pink elephant. Children are playing in the next room, and you suddenly realize that they are being really quiet. You ask them, "Are you okay next door?" They reply, "Yes, Mum, we are not drawing on the walls!" Umm… they're drawing on the walls… By using a negative such as "not," it means the opposite to the recipient.

"I promise you I am not like this normally" umm… to the recipient, you are like this normally, and the trust can be broken. Even subliminally, the negatives can reinforce the message. He calls the negatives (not, can't, don't, won't, etc.) a pink elephant and teaches you how to drop all of your pink elephants in your communication. It's a lot more challenging to do once you realize how much negative language you use, but it's also fun to do, and it really works. Your communication becomes more precise, efficient, empowering, and powerful.

If you take it a step further, your self-talk is the same. How many times do you use a negative word such as "wouldn't," "didn't," "haven't," "never," etc.? The main one being on time management: "I didn't do that, what an idiot!" I mean, seriously! Has that had such an impact that you need to review your whole life around what you didn't do??? Like my boss used to say, we are far from being brain surgeons; we are okay to make a mistake and forget or being too busy on that day to achieve what we had planned.

There is also a chapter on what I call chocolate language, how your sentences can entice the audience for more rather than being plain simple. I love trying to find new chocolate language to engage my audience. Most of the time, getting them to imagine or reflect on something they would feel is the best way.

We teach this at reception level: when a customer calls for an appointment this afternoon and you know you have none left for the day, instead of saying "no sorry we're fully booked" (which can make the customer feel like you'd rather they go somewhere else), we say "Of course, let me have a look for you. Unfortunately, we are fully booked today, but I can add you to the waiting list if something opens up. Alternatively, I have a 10 am appointment available on Thursday. How does that sound?"

I mean, that's so much better for the customer to feel like you can and want to solve their appointment issues, right?

I recommend a book to everyone I meet that changed my perspective on communication and allowed me to be more precise in what I want to say. Too often, we assume we've communicated properly, but have we?

One of my favorite quotes is "The single biggest problem in communication is the illusion that it has taken place" by George Bernard Shaw.

I always used to ask my managers, when they confronted an issue, to take a step back and think before acting on frustration or exasperation: "How did you communicate? Was that communication effective? Was it too sporadic? Was it assumed?" If you can analyze and critique what you've done and feel satisfied with the way you've approached it, then the issue is on them.

I equally hate blame culture as it does nothing for the business and everyone else involved. However, I do this exercise purely to ensure that my leadership is on point and to consider how I could handle situations better next time. A good leader will reflect rather than going all gun blazing, and 90% of the time, it's miscommunications that occur.

I once delivered a leadership course for managers in a family-run hotel. The chef had been working there since the beginning of time, and when I dug down further into what was happening, it became apparent that the hotel was run by emails. Everything was email-based, which created a culture of non-communication, and as long as I put it on email, it's dealt with. He was frustrated. One day, he received an email in the morning during breakfast, saying that a party of ten people were coming for lunch, and the requirements of their food were as such. He only read it at 11am after breakfast had ended, so the pressure to deliver something ultra-specific for 12pm really got to him. "How difficult is it for someone to come and see me and ask me if that's possible instead of assuming that it's okay and sending me an email so they can wipe their hands of responsibilities?" There you have it, now we can blame the chef for delivering something that had nothing to do with the requirements expected from these guests and always being a grumpy so-and-so for moaning at everyone. But I agree with him, any form of communication that creates such a ripple effect of negativity is never healthy and generates a culture that unless broken, will cause frustration and unfairness. We tried to change it, but it came from the top… too busy to work it out differently, so the only way to generate something better for the chef was for him to have a meeting with the head of each department in the morning so communication was clearer between them.

When one of my managers said to me regarding something quite major that we wanted to implement in the spa: "But I told them at the team meeting, and it's on the monthly memo, I keep repeating myself, it's annoying." My answer to him was: "If you keep repeating yourself, it means that there is something in your communication that is inefficient." To me, if it's that important, I would put it in the memo, have an individual meeting with each of them to go through it, have them sign the memo, and reiterate my news at a team meeting. Then if someone is oblivious to the change, I can deal with that person and manage them as my communication on this instance was flawless.

When managing a team, becoming more assertive and precise in your words becomes essential. If you say everything that is in your head, you will engage the team in your stress and tribulations. Having a senior member of staff you can trust and speak freely to is important, and for those who can't, having a coach or a mentor will allow you to offload. Your communication to your team becomes more focused on essentials and being able to manage expectations with better focus. "Let me think about it and come back to you" was one of my most favorite sentences as it allowed me to have time to think of the answer and be less reactive, which can send negative connotations to the team.

We will go through the tools of communications later on in the book.

→ BODY LANGUAGE

Body language is the most impactful form of communication.

Many experts in body language are possibly against these %s but the fact of the words being less impactful remains a reality nonetheless.

Regardless, let me share what I believe are the % of what communication is formed of[3]:

55% Body language
38% Tone of voice
7% Words

So basically, if your body language or tone of voice isn't correct, no one will take notice of your words. When you meet someone for the first time, you instantly decide whether you like or dislike them. Despite them just standing there, it's their energy and body language that cause you to make this decision. It's the small details that are the most important, such as adopting open body language to diffuse situations and settle disagreements. Having your palms visible when you talk, keeping your arms uncrossed, and making strong eye contact are a few positive actions that you can take right away.

———

I wrote this blog a while ago which has been a topic of many webinars and modules or one to one coaching:

5 WAYS TO GET MORE COMFORTABLE WHEN GIVING EMPLOYEE FEEDBACK

One of the best gifts a leader can give its team is honest employee feedback. When done constructively and helpfully, it can have a substantial impact on engagement levels. But there is one widespread problem, and it's called "feedback phobia". From both the management and employee sides, the process is often perceived as an uncomfortable 'thing'. The truth is, giving feedback to your staff can be tricky: it's not always easy to stay neutral in the conversation. But that doesn't mean there aren't ways to change that.

Taking The Dread Out Of Giving Employee Feedback.

Throughout my years of managing large teams, I have realised that there are five key points to become more comfortable in giving feedback. If, like me, you have many years of experience managing staff, you might be familiar with some of the following points. However, for the first-time manager, this is study material!

1. The Environment

I once sat in a coffee place, only to hear a manager talking to an employee and giving her feedback on her lack of teamwork. 'The poor staff member', I kept thinking, as it was quite demeaning for her. Having a coffee with your staff member is fine but consider what type of feedback you need to give. For what I heard that day, this would have been better in their office!

Choosing the right environment for the chat is crucial. Personally, I've always adopted this strategy:

Good feedback = On the shop floor

Constructive feedback = Away from the business, perhaps in a coffee shop and in a quiet corner

Tricky feedback = In the office

Consider asking your employee where they'd feel comfortable: "Where would you want to talk? I just need five minutes of your time."

2. Body Language

Possibly the most important aspect of giving feedback: 55% of the communication is non-verbal. For you to become comfortable giving employee feedback, I strongly suggest assessing your surroundings, as it affects your body language. Make sure there are zero barriers between the both of you – like a desk, for instance. The desk, or whatever is between you both for that matter, makes the meeting more formal, and this should be used for disciplinary meetings.

In a cafe, try to find somewhere where there is a small table or a sofa. This allows you to have an 'open' body language, meaning that you have nothing to hide or no second agenda in mind.

Listening is an art, so you must nod and acknowledge your employee's point when it's necessary. Also, keep in mind these three important rules of body language:

→ Your palms should be on show

→ Remember that your smile is important

→ Make eye contact.

Consider learning more about body language by listening to podcasts, reading books or articles on it! It's fascinating what you can discover!

3. "Hot Dog" Communication

When giving employee feedback, the hot dog communication approach works wonders: Bread – Sausage – Bread. Using the hot dog conversation style allows you to communicate better:

The bread = Think of something positive to say

Sausage = The feedback

The bread = Finish on a positive note

Some people call it a different sandwich, but basically, every conversation should go like this: positive, negative, and positive. If you adopt this method, you will find that it allows you to start and finish on a positive note, which will make your staff feel more motivated and less deflated.

Consider writing down key positive points before your meeting so you remember to mention them, and practice this method in all areas of your life to get used to this way of communicating.

I remember my managers saying that they had nothing good to say about Flossy, so how can I even apply this sandwich? But there is always something good to say about Flossy! They are usually the ones who are performing the best, hence why they usually become Flossy! So here is an example: "Flossy, your columns are fully booked. I am always amazed at how you manage to achieve that. I wanted to mention it since last month was particularly strong. I want to bring to your attention, however, the fact that there are a few concerns in the room."

Discuss the room and find solutions together: "Thank you, that was great. I trust that we are coming to an understanding, and we will visit the room daily before you leave. I am sure this will put a stop to this. Again, well done for last month, and let's move forward from now on."

4. Get Them To Talk

Communication goes both ways. It's important that your staff gets a chance to speak so you clear everything out and iron the issues before they leave. Ask questions, reiterate their points by confirming what they have said, and confirm the outcome so you both agree. It's crucial that their point of view is heard, regardless of how wrong they are. Listening and coming up with a solution that you both agree on is a win-win situation.

Consider asking questions straight away to get them talking: "How did it go with the customer yesterday?" Put them at ease before getting into the core of the chat.

5. Business Needs

At the end of the day, everything comes down to the business' needs. If you have this at the back of your mind when giving employee feedback and listening to your team, the outcome of the meeting is straightforward enough. In other words: "How does this impact the business' needs?"

This allows you to become neutral, listen to everything that is said, and be calm when making decisions. I have heard and witnessed many situations in which managers became too personal (just like the one in the coffee shop). Keep in mind that it's not about you, it's about what the business needs in order for it to be represented as the top brand that you have built.

Consider a team meeting where you go through your salon or spa's needs. Usually, you can do that as you analysing the customer journey with them. They will quickly understand what the business needs in order to reach its full potential.

This blog was specific in revisiting communication and where it takes place. I remember a staff member coming into the spa looking tired and fed up. My manager saw it too and followed her to the staff room to ask if she was okay. Why do this while she is changing and getting ready and with everyone coming in and out of the staff room? My manager stood there with her arms crossed, and although her voice was sympathetic, her body language was saying otherwise. Of course, the staff member's answers were short and blunt: "I'm okay, thanks."

I waited until we delivered the morning hub meeting and asked the staff member to come with me to her room. I sat down on her chair, and she sat down on the customer's chair. Our eyes were at the same level, but more importantly, there was nothing between us, so the communication was very much open. I simply asked, "We have worked together for some time now, and I can see that you might be going through something or something has possibly annoyed you. You know we are here to support you, and you can choose to keep what is happening to yourself, but right now, what can I do to support you?" Her voice was trembling, and it turned out that she was splitting up from her cheating boyfriend and was in a terrible headspace. We gave her a couple of days off when we could to take time to recenter, and although she was quite private and unable to share the whole story, she knew we would be there to help her when needed.

Another example is when we do mystery shopping, and the therapist sits us down in a huge chair while standing up and asking us questions. Not only does it feel like we are unable to open up to them, but it is also quite intimidating. So be very mindful of your surroundings and body language. It truly is what matters the most, and your body language becomes one of the most important aspects of communication. When I needed to have a stern word, it was always in the office with the desk between us so that there was a barrier that allowed them to know I was unhappy just by the way they walked in.

. . .

→ ACTIVE LISTENING

Listening is key to perfect communication. However, active listening can be difficult, especially for a busy leader with many things on their mind. Having that many tabs open in your mind can make it challenging to concentrate, yet active listening is the only way to have a positive impact on your communication with others.

When you are listening, body language is crucial. Consider maintaining eye contact and nodding to reinforce the fact that you are listening intently.

When listening, remember three key elements that you are being told and ask relevant questions about them. It's a given fact that when you're offered the chance to explain more, you feel like you are being listened to.

So pay attention: Give the speaker your undivided attention, and acknowledge the message by nodding and confirming what they have said. Show that you are listening with your body language, but also mirror their language. If someone speaks to you about their clients, use the same word so they know you have listened, even subconsciously. If you use the word "client," it will not align with them and will plant a seed of doubt in their mind. If they are talking about Mrs. Smith, then reiterate that name.

Provide feedback to engage them in the conversation, but most importantly, never judge, as that's a personal opinion. You can give your personal opinion if someone asks for it, but otherwise, avoid words such as "I think" or "I believe." This will only make the recipient feel inappropriate in their behavior.

Ensure the questions you are using are open-ended questions to get the conversation flowing. The more you make them talk, the more they feel listened to. Open-ended questions start with: "What," "When," "How," "Why," "Who," "Where," and "Tell me."

Tell me, when did that happened?
Where do you think it would be better to do this?
How did that make you feel?
Why did you react that way?
Where do you think this could be happening?
What makes you so annoyed with this situation?
Who decided this matter?

By staying neutral and avoiding reactions, and by being passive in your listening, you will find that people open up more. You can have an opinion, but making someone realize their action will be far more powerful than telling them: "I am the owner, I know the answer." It's down to them to tell you.

When you close a conversation, it's when you use closed questions such as "do you," "have you," "did you?" These generate a yes or no answer. Open-ended questions allow you to focus on the other person, and everyone loves to talk about themselves. Showing them different ways of thinking gives them options they can choose, rather than you imposing your opinions on them.

I remember very early on in my career working behind the counters in a London department store, one of the ladies who worked with me took a shine to me and taught me so much when it came to communication. We were at lunch one day in the canteen, and someone she knew came to sit with us. She started talking, my colleague started asking her open-ended questions, focusing on her and getting her to reveal so much. At the end of the conversation, the lady stood up and said: "Thank you so much. That was the best lunch I ever had. I needed that chat!"

When she left, I asked my colleague if she knew the lady well. She said: "Valerie, I barely know her. I did a stocktake with her many moons ago, but for some reason, she tells me everything about her life. And that's because I ask questions and am interested. The key to active listening is to get them to talk, ask questions, ask more questions, and never speak about yourself. She left feeling amazing and that I am so lovely to speak to. She knows nothing about me, nothing about my opinion, she just needed to talk and offload. Let them do that, and they will think you are amazing."

That experience will stay with me forever. Knowing that, as a leader, you can empower someone purely on active listening and being interested in their perspectives rather than yours.

→ CONFIRMING

Confirm what you have been told from at least three key aspects of the conversation. This reassures the person you are talking to and will help them to listen to you better. It's important to confirm the most important aspect of their conversation, but the key is to give them solutions: "What if you do it this way? How about thinking of it this way? When you do this, what consequences can it have?"

The aim is to get them to nod or agree. When the person nods or says yes, you have confirmed that you understand them. Giving them solutions becomes easy as they trust your thought process. Again, it's important to focus on a solution-finding mindset rather than offering a personal opinion.

The same principles apply to communication over the phone. Active listening can be difficult, so it's helpful to use phrases like "yes, of course" and ask questions. Nothing is an issue, so a solution-finding mindset is crucial. The more you engage in the conversation, the more they will reveal. If you focus on the three main concerns, you can zoom in on those and make the person feel heard.

One day, I asked my daughter to make a mystery phone call to a spa where I was going to deliver training. She called and said she wanted to treat her mum to a lovely experience. The receptionist assumed it was just for one person and never considered the possibility of it being for two since my daughter sounded young. As a result, she completely dismissed the opportunities for additional treats that my daughter asked for.

Active listening can create opportunities. By confirming the needs of the person in front of you, you can have clear communication and engage them in finding solutions.

→ BE CONSISTENT

Consistency in your communication creates a long-lasting impact. People know you're approachable and able to deal with situations while remaining professional at all times, whether it's with colleagues or customers. Professionalism goes a long way.

From the team's perspective, knowing that you are steady in your emotions and always in the same mindset will allow trust to grow and generate a stronger impact on their mood than you think.

I learned the hard way, being French and emotional, in my early days as a manager. I used to cry in front of my team or be moody when I was going through a hard patch, especially with my bosses. One day, I heard one of my team members say, "Oh, she always cries and is emotional, so keep your moods to yourself."

This was a lightbulb moment when I realized that as a leader, it's okay to show your vulnerability and admit when you're messing up on something, but when it comes to wearing your heart on your sleeves, sharing too much information or showing every emotion that you're going through, it goes against you. It shows instability and a lack of consistency in growing the team the way you truly want.

I started being coached, reading books on leadership, and being more consistent in my focus. Sharing issues became more of a management time to focus on a solution-finding mindset. I then became more steady with my approach, focusing on them rather than me, and the support flooded in. When you have the attitude of "I give them everything, surely they should be happy," it never works this way. In fact, it goes against you.

"Kill them with kindness" is my motto. It will become apparent that you're able to deal with anything and your communication simply reassures them.

In all, communication allows you to generate a smooth operation and also a professional atmosphere which has a positive impact on both customers and staff.

It is important to understand that your communication is the key to your success.

Of course Steven Bartlett's podcast is excellent to listen to - so many great leaders to feel empowered by!

Learn to Delegate Efficiently

A system isn't a system if it relies on one person. As simple as that.

Delegation is a necessity if you want to grow in your business, however it is a discipline and a procedure that must be followed for it to be successful and give you a piece of mind.

Delegation is and will always be the heart of true leadership and one of the main soft skill to develop, especially for our Micromanagers out there.

Before we start, let's look at why we delegate?

→ It allows you to focus on bigger things to grow the business like networking

→ You are able to have a day off without feeling obliged to do "things" for the business constantly

→ It develops your staff on what they love to do or never knew they liked doing (that is true leadership!)

→ It engages your staff in your business

→ It generates more work achieved for your business to have a smooth operation

→ It helps with your time management so you can handle various tasks and oversee projects

What stops us?

→ It's hard to let go of what we do because we think "it's easier and quicker if I do it myself"

→ We have trust issue with the people around us

→ We think that we always have to double check therefore there are no points in delegating

→ We only delegate to the one who is keen to help

→ We don't know what to delegate

The issue with the lack of delegation is that everything relies on you. Even if you are away on holiday, you end up having to work on things that you shouldn't do anymore or come back to a mountain of things that no one dealt with.

The second issue is that your to-do list becomes endless which in itself is very stressful and overwhelming.

The third one is that you micro-managing everything which can be extremely deflating for your team and create an atmosphere of miss-trust.

How do you delegate?

→ Firstly, you need to know why you are delegating and that it will take a little time to get it right. If you accept that there will be mistakes then you are ready do delegate and take your business to another level.

→ The second aspect of delegation is that you need to understand everyone's strength and weaknesses... there is 0 point delegating something to someone if they hate doing that. Making your team responsible allows makes the business run smoothly.

→ The third and most important is to understand that delegation will support your time management. With delegation, you will be able to have more time for yourself to grow your business or even for your personal development. The question to ask yourself is: what will I use the time for?

Then you are ready for the process:

→ Do a list of things you could delegate or don't have the time to do or grown out of

→ Have a team meeting, ask them to create a list of everything that has to be done in the business

→ Ask who would want to do what to engage them

→ Have your individual meetings straight away after this team meeting and explain your expectations. Set up the next follow up meetings.

→ The key to delegation is to ensure that you follow up. Without following up, it will be a recipe for disaster. If it's important to you, it will be important to them. If they feel you keep canceling your follow up meeting with them, they will not care simply because they feel that you don't care. Every time you delegate, if you fail to give them a deadline date, you will find that it will never be done or three months down the line, you are talking about the same task which defeats the object of delegation and will only breed frustration; For example, you could choose someone to run a team meeting as long as they feel followed through that process, it's an amazing way to develop them.

→ Accept that they might not get it right straight away but your follow up meetings are there to point them to the right direction. Discuss the solutions and what could be better if they did it another way

→ Change tasks if you can quarterly to give them room for growth and other things to do so boredom doesn't settle, however, be aware of their skills. If someone hates counting, there is little point to give them the stocktake to do but perhaps, they are more the creative type and would love to help you create an event

→ Create the most impactful delegation by giving feedback and acknowledgement when things are done efficiently, constructive feedback can be so empowering

→ Adopt a delegation mentality from the start (at recruitment level) as everyone will know your expectations and that when you come and work here, you are not, "Just a hairdresser/therapist/team member."

What if?

→ If no one comes forward: then you know the kind of team you have. With your individual meetings, delegate the tasks yourself. You will know your flossy's and the ones that are never bothered. It's then a matter of management.

→ If everyone wants to do the same task: do the task as a team effort rather than individually. For example, no one wanted to deal with the stock I ended up making it a team effort once a month where we all had a mask on and counted as a team with pizza to support us! In the end, everyone was looking forward to it...

→ If they keep making mistakes: maybe you didn't delegate the right task to this person but make sure if it's not an attitude issue which will need to be managed through your performance management procedure.

Delegation is part of your management skills that will develop your leadership skills and in the long run give you freedom. The bottom line is that to keep your work/life balance, you must delegate to feel better and focused in your tasks.

Having a team that understands their work doesn't stop at their stations/rooms/own tasks allows you to grow as a business.

No matter how painful the start is, once your work is delegated, all you will have to do is schedule follow up meetings (otherwise they will not happen) to ensure the tasks are done and set your expectations but you will be able to leave your business without worrying and have a decent holiday as you know things are being done. It will also go down to your structure and whether you have the right people in the right position.

We will revisit this later on in this book.

The Key Soft Skills Since the Pandemic

Of course, these soft skills are valid for your leadership to grow, however, they have never been so valuable since the first ever lockdown. We have had to make so many ethical business decisions that are still happening now and these two soft skills allow you to overcome various situations whilst thinking of the good of your employees and business.

1. Flexibility

When we talk about "flexibility," it usually means the ability to adapt to changes, which is why the pandemic was a huge test of this soft skill. Being flexible when it comes to work matters a lot, but it's also true on a personal level. Flexibility is a crucial soft skill because it demonstrates an ability and willingness to take on new tasks and challenges with patience and without feeling stressed or overthinking everything. Flexibility is a soft skill that micromanagers find very hard to consider when making decisions.

Before the pandemic, I was a consultant for seven years, and in 2019, I was the busiest I had ever been. Even though everything was on my shoulders, I knew I needed to invest in employing a few people to support my growth. But like any business and its growth, the day-to-day was overtaking everything, and I was very busy traveling internationally, doing my social media, all of my admin, and recruiting new clients. My reputation was and still is of someone effective and serious, but I knew that what I was telling my clients should have been reflected in my own business. When someone makes their business look easy, it usually hides a huge amount of work to make it as smooth as it seems. So I only know too well that my days were unbalanced, but my vision was simple: building a team of experts and having various aspects of my business grow that would all rely on others.

Before the pandemic hit the UK hard in March 2020, I hired a marketing strategist, Laura Sarao (who founded 'Wild For Dogs' - check her out on Instagram), in January 2020. She was working one day a week to rebrand and create an online platform that would take on some of my new clients and allow me to stop traveling so much. Everything was going to be launched in July 2020. I started to interview various people for admin, coaching, and content support. And although I never found what I was looking for, I was determined to grow and allow my vision to take shape. I believe that the growth of a business that is steady and strategized has more of a chance to survive for the long term.

Then, of course, the lockdown in March 2020 put all of us on standstill. I remember having countless conversations with clients, people I knew in the industry, and starting to create webinars, support networks, and focus on everything that I could do to help. Laura was brilliant, and I thank her to this day for her incredible help as it would have taken me much longer had I been on my own. I am a strong believer in things happening for a reason. We called each other and said, "We need everything yesterday!" The wheel was in motion with a website with new branding, webinars, blogs, posts, support calls for anyone who was struggling, and we were ultra-focused. Time was of the essence.

Like many, I saw my future business disappear before my eyes. As many members were canceling their membership for fear of the unknown, which I understood, given that February 2020 was the busiest month I had ever had, the future looked very uncertain indeed.

I worked so hard. One of my daughters was in Thailand and was confined there in a hotel near the beach, the best place for her to stay. London, UK had a different feel, and staying here with my youngest daughter, we created our own little safe house and went through the motions. I mean, *what on earth do they hear at that age?* I remember thinking. 20 years old, and she must need reassurance. I have years of experience to overcome emotions, so I was focused. We talked a lot, so her mind was reassured, and she built her art studio downstairs, so our little habits became so comforting in a world that became hostile. But life goes on, and the mindset that I had forged so many years ago became my comfort. Visualizing and meditation helped me and continue to do so. I highly recommend it.

I decided that I had nothing to lose and worked ultra-hard with Laura to create everything I wanted to put out there. I guess the pandemic, despite its intensity, had a silver lining. Like many others, we had time to revisit everything and dissect the business so it could become a stronger, sleeker one.

A month into the lockdown, I decided that my laptop needed to go to sleep for a long weekend as I was exhausted. I had little time to think, so time out was necessary at that stage.

I called my dear mother, and since she is a psychologist, she said to me something that really helped to unblock all of my uncertainty:

"We need to mourn the old ways of doing things; we need to say goodbye to how we used to work as we are entering a new phase. In fact, the whole world is entering a new phase. With mourning, comes seven phases:

Shock - Denial - Anger - Bargaining - Depression - Acceptance - Processing Grief

Some people will never come out of this pandemic alive, so we ought to be grateful for our health and future. But know that mourning for you at this stage is purely a way of life. Out of the seven stages, anger is the one to look out for, and if you avoid dealing with it, it will come back to you in the form of depression, eating disorders, or even illness. You must get that anger out. I suggest doing a big poster with corona virus written on it. Put it outside in the garden on the wall, take your boxing gloves, and both of you go and punch it as hard as you wish."

"But anger is far from what I feel. I just want to help as many people as I can with what I know," I proclaimed.

"It's crucial that you do it as right now, even if you feel that the anger is deep down inside of you, you had zero time to process everything that has just happened. Just do it and release that anger," she insisted.

Okay, Mum, I get it, but come on! As a psychologist, you're telling me to go out and punch a poster with "coronavirus" written on it! "Nothing to lose, everything to gain, flexible mindset in gear," we did just that and had a good laugh with it. Nothing much happened that day, but that weekend, I was meditating, the first time I managed to give myself the time and take a step back, and something came to me: I never have to travel again unless I want to. Everything will be digitized.

That was it. Everything became much clearer. My vision became stronger, and my mindset was at ease: my sole mission alongside Laura's was to build a business that would be solely online and attract other experts in the industry. I had already been working with Terri Irvin, my amazing Retail & Mindset Coach for three years by then and loved empowering others in retail sales. Building from that, it would be the natural path to continue growing the business. In two months, I was able to support more people than ever. Four months later, Amy Gordon came to join me. Eight months later, there were ten of us working on various projects and aspects of the business.

I remember never panicking and being ultra-calm, even strangely calm through it all. Focusing on my vision, which I had had a long time ago, it only felt possible now. I realized that being flexible on what was coming through every day, from the news to clients' mindsets, I needed to be flexible enough to overcome challenges and difficult times.

Listening to so many situations, the ones that were suffering the most were the ones that had a mindset stuck in their day-to-day and unable to see how it could be worked out differently. Enter Micromanagers, trying to change their mindset so they could survive, became one of my strengths, and clients kept coming through for that one-to-one support. I knew that coaching in a group would be more cost-effective, but it's the one-to-one support that I loved and still love now. We all have a need for that critical friend once in a while, especially in business, as many around us are unable to fully understand what we are going through. So being able to carry on being that was so important to me, especially when helping more owners since online meeting platforms allowed me to do so. To really be flexible, we must work on our solid foundations and ethos first. Hence, why I believe that you need to have an operation that is completely set, and your core values never truly change. They keep you grounded in what you represent.

But being open-minded to change and tweaks there and then to make your life easier is important to allow flexibility to take shape. There is an element of trust and optimism that is needed in flexibility, but I really despise the word "positive." One of the reasons is that it's pure pressure: "I must be positive" seriously! Enough already! We have enough pressure, so thinking NLP or thought process is a lot more effective and gentle to the mindset and more realistic in our constant pursuit of work-life balance. I sympathized so much with my clients who had to homeschool their young children. I knew that was a challenge in itself, never mind having to stay afloat while all of this was going on. The world became reactive to everything, mindset was compromised by the daily news, and our support became more and more important to reinforce. We were in full swing, "Come and cry on my shoulders, offload your worries," this became our sole mission.

Two elements that really helped in my flexibility were staying calm and planning ahead. As I said, I was strangely calm. Perhaps it was all of the years of experience that taught me to keep the panic at bay, or maybe it's because of living in the UK for over 30 years that allowed me to be more pragmatic, or it is because I believe in what I do. I just want to help and support as many people as I could, so the mission became crystal clear.

There is an element of assessment of the challenges. Somehow being able to view the issue from all angles will allow you to be less one-sided. There are always different aspects to an issue. You just have to sit and think about it rather than be reactive. Pro-activeness can be taught through the systems in place. Once you have reviewed all approaches to the challenge, you will find solutions that are more rounded, more aligned with what you believe. After all, everything is never all black and white.

I have met countless owners that have been flexible enough to work differently and listen to different ways of doing things. Now, my members are doing so well, numbers they have never achieved before as they are so busy. But most of all, most of them have taken a step back and are working on the business, making the business work for them rather than working for the business 24/7.

If I had to define flexibility, to me, it is a crucial soft skill to focus on. It allows you to ride the waves and helps you overcome situations. After all, it's never all plain sailing, there is always something that will require your attention. It's how you ride that wave that will make the most impact on a professional and personal note. To me, flexibility becomes your only strength to overcome your challenges and overcomes micromanagement. Once you have learned that flexibility of mind, your leadership will become stronger. You might even be doing it now but are completely unaware of it. Focus on your conscious thoughts: there is always a solution to a challenge. As simple as that. Our mind will play tricks and send us to the dark alley of despair. Be mindful and aware, it's the only way that flexibility will grow, and ultimately, you will become the leader you dreamt of.

2. Resilience

Then comes resilience.

Funnily enough, when I wrote this sentence, I wrote "resistance" which is what you must work on to overcome and be open to change and tweaks to make your workload better. Resistance could be the opposite of resilience in that instance. Resilience makes you overcome challenges in a healthy, more proactive way as your mindset stays strong and focused.

By definition, resilience is the ability to bounce back after life tears you down. Those who are more resilient have learned to move past obstacles and challenges and know how to weather the storms that come along.

So how do you become resilient? Building strong and positive relationships, having a support network is crucial. Too often in the pandemic, in particular, I have seen the support network being ultra-toxic and advising my clients to step away from it all. I advised them to focus on what I told them to focus on so they felt better in their business and then go back to the support network if they wanted to, better armed with their mindset and systems. Often, they were left feeling inadequate and comparison being the thief of joy, was counteracting their hard work. Be mindful of that, you should never feel bad from your support network but elevated.

I also believe that making everyday count and being present in the moment is priceless. 'The Power of Now' by Eckhart Tolle helped me years ago to enjoy the delights of the day-to-day life, and I believe it makes you more resilient to changes. You appreciate more. Gratitude is also so crucial; I journal and practice gratitude every day. This makes you feel humble and hopeful, and to me, far more powerful than saying, "I must be positive".

Self-care has a lot to answer for, from mindset to habits, they are the key to your day-to-day mindset and feel: it's all about the details.

But most of all, I believe that resilience means being proactive rather than reactive. Ask yourself: what is the issue and what are the solutions I can have? As I mentioned, there are always more than one solution, and taking a well-rounded approach will allow you to feel confident in your solution.

There are always many solutions to a problem, and once you make a choice, it's the right one because it made sense to you at the time. Proactivity allows you to overcome a problem before it even becomes one. That's exactly why having a business with a clear defined structure and systems will eventually help you see where potential problems may arise.

→ She is going to get married so will need three weeks off - what solutions do I have to cover her shifts?

→ We are getting a lot of calls at reception level - what solutions do I have to that?

→ This particular treatment is popular and I should have more people delivering it - what solutions do I have to that?

→ The managers are unable to handle their work and taking it home which is against my ethos in promoting work-life balance - what solutions do I have to that?

→ I want to go away for a month and travel - what solutions do I have to that?

You get the gist… Proactivity allows you to become more resilient to changes that could happen, flexibility allows you to overcome those challenges that often are tricker than predicted.

I guess that you become more resilient with more experience and learning from these experiences becomes crucial. Often, we beat ourselves for things that we did incorrectly, but with time, all of this passes. Assessing what we have done, what happened and how we reacted to it is crucial to grow and become resilient. We all mess up once in a while, stand up, dust yourself off and carry on… the British mentality really has rubbed off on me over the years!

I was looking at quotes for resilience, these rang true to my heart:

> *"I can be changed by what happens to me. But I refuse to be reduced by it."* - Maya Angelou

> *"Resilience is accepting your new reality, even if it's less good than the one you had before. You can fight it, you can do nothing but scream about what you've lost, or you can accept and try to put together something that's good."* - Elizabeth Edwards

> *"Do not judge me by my success, judge me by how many times I fell down and got back up again."* - Nelson Mandela

Confession Time!

During the pandemic, Marc was working around the clock on his business and eventually reached a state of burnout. One day, while in lockdown, he admitted that he was struggling to focus on all areas of his business. He was aware that he didn't want to bother his team, as they were on furlough and there seemed to be no point in taking them out of it to help him. When I asked why, he explained that he thought they would never be able to do what he does, so what's the point of trying to train someone? Although Marc's cash flow was healthy enough to hire at least one person to help him out, he was reluctant to do so. I advised him that he had no choice but to get help. We spoke to one of his staff members who had returned from furlough to assist him, and eventually, Marc was ready to listen to the structure that I knew would change his old ways.

---

1. https://www.mindthesolution.be/the-rice-experiment/
2. TLEX Institute - 'Mind Matters: How To Effortlessly Have More Positive Thoughts' (March 2023)
3. 'Drop The Pink Elephant' - Bill McFallen (2003)

5

BUILDING TRUST

Operational Road Map

Now it's crunch time. At the end of the day, only the customer journey matters and building your Operational Road Map consists of two aspects:

→ Customer journey

→ Staff journey

Only once this is defined can you truly build your structure and start letting go of the day to day to build the bigger picture.

A. Let's focus on your customer journey:

I invite you to analyze your customer journey, which ultimately will allow you to examine your operation and highlight what can be improved, what's missing, and what's good. I call it the Good, the Bad, and the Ugly of the customer journey. It's time to be honest and become your own critic. Saying that, it's also an interesting exercise to do with your team, as their opinion is valuable; after all, they are working and seeing everything themselves. That's leading by sharing and making their values.

One exercise that is brilliant to do with the team is this: separate them into three groups (smaller teams, you don't have to separate) and give them large pieces of paper. One to think of the customer journey before the customer enters the business, one to think of the customer journey during their visit, and one to think of the customer journey after their visit. Give them 15 minutes to brainstorm and write everything down on that large piece of paper. Each team then presents what they have found and discusses it with everyone else. You can all decide what the best customer journey is and ensure that everyone buys into it. It's such an interesting exercise to do and gets the team to have their input on the journey, and you might be surprised as to what they come up with.

Customer Journey analysis is extremely defined and crucial to review every single year. It prompts us to ask important questions: Are we still delivering the best service? Does our service align with our ethos? What challenges do we face in providing an exceptional customer journey? What feedback do we receive from our customers? Every aspect matters, from the initial phone call to the glass of water before treatment, from the retail area to the facilities. What do our customers see and feel throughout their experience? Are they so delighted that they want to return to us repeatedly? Paying attention to every detail is essential.

If you need further assistance in defining your customer journey and accessing a comprehensive analysis checklist, please visit www.thedelforgegroup.co.uk. Our course is specifically designed to support you in this area. As the heart of your business, let's ensure we get it right.

B: Now, let's focus on your staff journey:

Too often, when I am reading about leadership, it's about me and how I should develop my skills. But as mentioned, I like to look at something from all different angles to really make up my mind. This is something you must try to do from now on: never take the first answer at face value and think further.

I started to wonder how my leadership would affect the people around me. At each stage of their journey with me, how do they perceive my leadership? After all, I am leading them, so their feelings and emotions are important. Since they are all going to be following that one vision, that one dream, I must encourage them to trust me. Without trust, there is little leadership to be had.

Trust is gained, we know that. Rarely will we trust and respect someone just because they are the boss and are superior. Of course, I will obey what is being asked of me, but their leadership will get everything out of me. So I want to better and better myself constantly under them. If I feel flat as an employee or start distrusting the organization, it starts at the top. That leader matters, that leader I want to follow, or not.

Someone asked me once: do you only deal with businesses that have teams? What about the ones that work alone? Well, leadership is equally as important. You might not have a whole team around you to lead, but you still need to manage your time and workload between your accountant to your social media helper, passing from the cleaner to the stock delivery. Everything is leading towards the growth of yourself and your business. So the answer is that we focus on businesses of all sizes, as it always falls back to the same: structure, systems, and operation.

So, I started to think of how I impact them, and when does that start? How many stages are there in their journey with me?

Let me introduce you to the 7 Steps of Leadership.

1. RECRUITMENT

Ohhh... the dreaded recruitment! It's time-consuming, exhausting, and talk about putting your mindset back to flat. Let's never talk about those time-wasters! The point is that recruitment is a pain in "le derriere", pardon my French! Countless times we get bored with recruitment. Yet, it is the most important step that builds a relationship between the new potential comer, you, and your business.

So, we have to interview a lot of frogs to discover our prince, and that can play a significant impact on welcoming a new team member, so how we deal with it matters.

Most of all, I have seen some shock horrors when it comes to recruitment. Now, I know, we can blame this generation for being so difficult and indifferent, but you will find that my grandad thought the same with my dad's generation when, in the 60s, women were burning their bras in protest, and crisis was also in full swing in the 70s. Life was too challenging between generational clashes. So, every generation tends to dismiss and disagree with the generation that is coming through.

And of course, the pandemic on a global level, add Brexit to the UK, has made the whole recruitment crisis a lot more challenging. But again, being flexible and resilient, it's a matter of analyzing the business to work differently if the case needs to be. I have clients that downsized, so they never had to deal with such big teams ever again but understood that the remaining of their teams still need that leadership. I have clients that love working with their teams, and recruitment or not, they are stronger than ever because we flossed the Flossies and focus on high performers as well as employing newer staff members to focus on the smaller treatments, clever. I have clients who continue to empower others and revisited their opening hours to ensure the team worked together and stop trying to fill positions they are unable to.

All of the above is right as long as it aligns with you and your finances (hence the crucial aspect of your budget, which is what we help you with here at The Delforge Group®). It's the right solution.

I feel that as Leaders, we ought to take a part of the blame when it comes to recruiting. I have heard horror stories from a candidate perspective that will never empower anyone, let alone a younger generation:

→ Managers making the candidate wait for 30 minutes as they are busy

→ Interview in a cafe for everyone to hear

→ I once had a candidate being interviewed on an online platform by the whole team who were asking her so many personal questions, it was rather stressful for her and declined the offer.

→ A manager that agreed to be paid cash, only to be told sorry I can't afford you three weeks later and dismissed like a nobody

→ A candidate that had five interviews only to feel underwhelmed by the processes and chose something else in a different industry altogether

→ So many candidates never receiving feedback so they never know what to improve at interview level

→ A candidate that got the job, left her current employer, only to be told, "sorry I changed my mind," one week before employment so had no job to go to, how can she feel empowered?

→ A candidate that created a whole mood board and ideas only to be told no thank you but the mood board was never returned so her work was basically stolen as far as she was concerned.

You name it, we've heard it. It's always a 360-degree process when it comes to recruitment, and we must always look inward and revisit our processes. If you want to inspire, it should come from the recruitment process; otherwise, you could miss the one gem you have in front of you or make them feel inadequate and of no value. What's the point of that?

I remember when I was recruiting, I wanted to make sure that everyone I interviewed, whether I wanted them in the business or not, left feeling inspired. This not only helped to grow my reputation but also made my recruitment process more and more impactful.

When it comes to leadership, creating a procedure that allows you to have the same process with or without you in the business is crucial. Yes, I know it's hard enough to receive resumes/CVs, but it's always good to keep trying even if fully staffed. Why? Because you're looking for talent and long-term recruitment rather than panicking when someone leaves.

The key to recruitment is to avoid desperation. The new generation wants to see your business as an entity in its own right. Creating a powerful advertisement involves showing them how you work and the benefits of working for you. In all, just be yourself to attract the people who want to work for you.

We have discussed at length with various owners the disengagement happening in the world from potential staff members, and finding people who actually want to work for you is a real challenge. Unfortunately, I am unable to give you a solution for this. All I know is that being passionate, yourself, and focused as a leader will empower others. But if it fails to do so, the main thing is to align with who you are, as you will always find solutions. Even if you have to stop your business tomorrow due to the rise in costs and lack of recruitment, your leadership will never stop, as everything you have learned will be transferable to other opportunities in your life.

It is crucial to bear in mind that you are in charge of your own destiny, and your mindset will be the only friend that will help you overcome any situations thrown at you.

2. PROBATION

Ok, let's assume for a moment that you have managed to hire and your wonderful staff is starting in a week's time, fingers crossed, of course!

The managers should create a strong probation program for the length of the probation, which can vary between three to six months.

I am a huge fan of a welcome pack for my new staff member. Now, a few of my clients told me they send the contract alongside the employee handbook. If you look at the employee handbook and all the formalities involved in it, it is the opposite of empowerment: "do this, do that, must adhere to this and that", all about the heavy-duty grievance procedure. Talk about putting fear into people, especially the new generation! I love something a little lighter. To me, the employee handbook and contract can be signed on the first day of employment, but to engage from the start, before they even set foot in your business, how about engaging them differently?

My daughter was looking for a job and managed to find one in a local clothes shop. At 21, it was just a job to get her through university. From the start, at the interview level, she felt something was a little off. The manager rescheduled her appointment three times, she was 20 minutes late for the interview, and asked her very few questions before giving her the job outright and setting her up for her first day with where she needed to go and timings.

On her first day, she arrived, waited for someone to tell her where to go, and finally, after an hour, she was taken to an office, asked to sign papers, explained what she would be doing: one hour in the changing room, one hour at the front, and one hour to rearrange the clothes and so on. Throughout the whole day, no one engaged with her, no one knew who she even was. When the manager had time, she would come and check up on her and told her to go for lunch. She was unaware or even told about the canteen and spent money outside.

Is that empowering? Did she feel welcome? Did she want to go back? Did she feel special?

Of course, you could argue that this is never going to be her full-time job forever, but why not? I started in the beauty industry unsure if it was for me but loved it because I was shown the ropes, so to speak. How can we engage anyone if they never feel welcome or even shown what is happening in the business? Too often in the beauty and hair industry, in particular, I have seen the first day being: "here is the room, here is the wax pot, here is what we do after for the client, you have someone in an hour".

Once upon a time, I used to send parcels to the newcomers with samples, a letter, a photo of the team, and who was doing what in the business. Of course, this became time-consuming and very costly! So now, a welcome pack can be a letter to engage and welcome them to the business without the official bits of the employee's handbook.

If we want to set ourselves apart from the competition, as a small business, we must revisit how we empower from the start which means:

→ Set up a welcome letter with an organigram explaining who is who, what do to expect on his/her/they first day, where is the best lunch, the rota, the training booked and a really nice signed by the owner letter. You could even give them the phone number of the manager in charge that day, where to go, a few bits on the story of the business and even a little photo of the team. Even encourage them to come and pick up a few samples with the retail book for them to familiar themselves with. I have a client who even created a video to send to the new starter, really empowering from the start.

→ Create a probation period calendar with key dates such as their half way probation, their training booked and anything relevant to their probation

→ For their first week, set up a budget for them and another team member (a different team member every day) and give them money to have lunch together

→ Create a team meeting to welcome them to the team

→ Prepare a strong training programme, be careful of giving too much during the probation as they might leave before so it's best to look at the first year of employment and focus on a training matrix to register their progress

→ Have training bonds in place, they are sometimes a grey area as to whether you will get your money back if they leave within a certain amount of time but they are a deterrent to your staff abusing the training programme: if they leave within three months, they owe 90% of the training booked, within six months, they owe 60%, within nine months, 30% and within twelve months they owe nothing.

→ Buddy up program is so powerful maybe that could be a really good way to engage them with senior team members that train them or take them to lunch according to your budget set aside for that

→ Mystery shops are great to give them feedback

The start of their journey with you is so important. It will set them up for success rather than failure. Once more, you are never responsible for their behavior. And if, as an employer, you can hand on heart tell yourself that you have done everything in your power to engage and train your newcomer, then you can be satisfied in your leadership skills. It is important to revisit what went wrong if someone leaves earlier so you can continue to reshape your welcome pack and the probation period. However, sometimes, it's simply down to them. You can never control their attitude, but you can control yours.

3. ROUTINE

Since recruitment is so difficult at the moment, it's crucial to empower your team and yourself to do more than just the day-to-day routine. That's why I'm a huge fan of Individual Development Plans and Team Building days. We encourage these with our members as they allow you and your team to be excited about the future, whether it's training or places you want to take them for team building.

Individual Development Plans

Just what they say on the tin - they're individual to each person. You can focus them on more training, stock management, or even just have a 30-minute chat each month with them. It's important to reflect on what they're currently achieving. For example, one of my hairdressers wanted every Tuesday off to attend Drama classes. I granted that as long as he achieved his targets and the team wasn't affected. I knew his role was going to be limited in time, so my motto is that while they're with me, I want to ensure they have an amazing time and feel empowered. Nothing is forever, and having a plan of action directed towards their capabilities is the best way to engage each of them and ensure that they're fully focused on what you want them to achieve.

This plan can take the format of a folder on your computer or a physical folder. As long as it's kept in a locked cupboard so no one else can have access for GDPR purposes, it's fine. It can be quite nice for them to have everything on there from training to notes. Although, online drives save the planet and can also keep all documents! We've created a spreadsheet that holds all of the essential information that we would want to go through with them. We also believe that it's an excellent tool for management if you need to deal with difficulties because it allows you to confirm what you've done with that employee over the course of their time with you.

Team Building Days

It can be disgruntling when you see your team is always needing to be engaged and it can certainly be very difficult to keep finding things that are interesting, however, if it's never on the table then the routine becomes just that. Breaking that routine will allow you to feel that you are giving back to them. So why not getting your diary out for the year ahead and start thinking outside of the box, here are some ideas from my wonderful clients that avoids the involvement of alcohol and going out for a meal, which is always nice but could be in a different environment or circumstances:

→ Mental health expert support

→ Gym flying which one of my client did and sounded amazing!

→ Retreats and spa days

→ Visit a town with hotel and evening booked

→ Hire a team building business

→ Visit the labs of your brand

→ Be trained by a top expert for the day

→ Training day with models and doing treatments on each other

Of course, this means you must know your budget to plan ahead and ensure that you are focusing on the right thing.

4. FOLLOW UPS

Now, that's where the crucial aspect of being a leader comes to light.

Leadership is ensuring that the communication with your staff and the managers is consistent. Without follow ups, the teams becomes disgruntled: "The owner is always busy" "they say that but will quickly will forget" "my meeting is always moved and canceled anyway" etc. etc.

So following up on everything that you do becomes the most important aspect of your leadership.

Just like when you are delegating (Chapter 4), if you never set deadlines or follow ups, you will be the leader that always promises but under-delivers. It's so important that the follow up are part of your diary and become your priority all of the time, every time.

With Your Managers

The key is to ensure that you are creating a flow when it comes to communication, which will allow your meetings to be more solution-driven rather than you just talking through your task at them, which I call "clipboard management".

To become the leader who follows up on delegated tasks, you must make meetings with your managers a routine, ideally once a week, on the same day and at the same time. It's best to schedule them early in the week to start the week afresh, but this depends on your rota setup.

For every meeting, you should have an agenda, or else it will diverge into everything else but what you really need to talk about.

A minimum of one hour is needed, two hours if necessary, and three hours if the meetings are efficient and focused. Following up with your managers will empower them to create a strong sense of direction and focus on what matters, allowing you to focus on building the business in other ways. This will also create a sense of development for them.

Put these meetings in your diary for the year ahead, even if you're on vacation. If you have more than one manager, the meetings still occur even if one of them is on holiday. This ensures that the meetings remain consistent and productive.

One of my team members is holding these meetings every Tuesday, as they are closed on Mondays. She is now using on online meeting room while her managers are physically in the business, as she feels that she is constantly disturbed when she is on-site. This setup keeps her focused, and it works well for everyone. However, it is essential to review the efficiency of these meetings annually and tweak them if necessary. For instance, when we evaluated the effectiveness of the meetings, we determined that she needed to attend the first meeting of the month to perform a general maintenance and detailed walkthrough to ensure that the standards are up to date and to check on their standards.

We discuss this topic extensively in our Management to Leadership Programmes, which focus on the communication strategies that you need to adopt with your managers to empower them and develop them into leaders, as well as creating a week-by-week agenda.

Of course, taking your managers away from their day-to-day duties could cost you money, and it could even impede their work. However, it is crucial to understand that by focusing on their work, you are creating a strong operation. The more supported they feel in their roles, the better leaders they become, and the more they believe that you are building a strong rapport with their work, the more they will deliver.

I have seen time and time again how the success of these meetings can lead to creating a work-life balance and generating a strong sense of purpose.

With Your Team

Communication with your team is the most important one as it allows you to iron out any issues that happen quickly, but it will also encourage everyone to follow the direction that you want to take. As a leader, it is time consuming to constantly be in meetings, so encourage a strong communication. Again, your meetings should be part of the weekly routine, here are a few examples:

→ Weekly or monthly meetings depending of the performance of your team

OR

→ Weekly meeting with the managers and each of the staff members for 15/20 min

→ Monthly meetings with the owner for 30 min

OR

→ Monthly meetings with the managers and each of the staff members for 30 min

→ Quarterly meetings with the owner for 30 min

The more you are regular with your communication, the more you are creating a strong bond and build trust.

Again, the agenda is key but most of all, the recording of these are crucial to ensure there is consistency in the communication. For example, we encourage with our members to keep their meetings in a spreadsheet with all of the notes of the meetings so if one of the manager is on holiday and another one is taking over that meeting, they have all of the information necessary. Same when you do your meetings, you will have all of the information under one document which facilitates the smooth communication.

You can record:

The achievements you want to record

The 5* reviews

Complaints

Sickness

Training

Notes

Again, having an online document allows you to never have to send the notes back and forth on emails, but also you never have to save them, as it does that automatically.

The key to these meetings is a connection, again, stop being that clipboard manager and engage the conversation by asking opened ended questions. Ask them to go through their numbers and talk about their best and most challenging moments they have had the previous week.

It's important to engage by creating trust and we will discuss how to manage those difficult situations.

. . .

➜ **RECAP**

So why your communication in your structure is important?

Before we start working with a client, we focus on communication and how it is represented in the business as more often than not, we find that the communication has a recursive effect on the team and even customers with unclear marketing messages, it is often very much linked.

➜ I despise communication on a certain mobile app: well, I guess I should say that I have a love hate relationship with it. Love it because its easy and allows you to communicate with everyone in a group, so for you it's easy and simple! But what effect do you have on the recipient? I was coaching a manager whom I felt was getting very overwhelmed and I was wondering why.. It was simple: she was getting constant messages from the owner thinking of something and messaging her; 6am, 10pm, anytime she thought of something, she wanted to share in case she forgot. When I confronted her with it, she said that for her, it's not to deal with it straight away but to do when she has time. Wanting to show she could handle anything, the manager was unable to do her normal tasks plus what was expected.

→ Find a solution to your communication such as an online drive document

→ Create a structure in when you are communicating with all of the meetings booked up for the year ahead, try it, it will make them a priority

→ What do you want to be communicated to you? Ensure that you are clear with your expectations and ask the managers to send it to you before the meeting if possible as it will make them ready for the meetings.

Efficient communication comes when:

→ Your meetings with your managers are streamlined (example of the weekly feedback form)

→ Keep a paper/online trail of all of your team meetings so you keep track of what has been said

→ The more you plan, the more you will create a strong message for the long term

→ Your individual meetings are as followed and become a priority

→ You always go to a meeting with an agenda

→ The more you focus on your follow ups, the more your leadership will flourish

. . .

Too often, we wait for that magical person, that manager that is going to be solving all of your problems but there is a huge danger to that… If that manager comes in and install all of what is needed and the owners is none the wiser, if they leave, you are back at square one. She can add to the systems but it has to be yours in the first place, otherwise, you are reliant on someone else and that is never healthy in the first place.

What if she leaves? The systems too? What if the systems are inefficient? You wasted a lot of time? It's time to input what you believe is key to the operation and that always starts with the follow ups: say what you do and do what you say. Most of all, does such manager actually exist?

5. DIFFICULTIES

Managing difficulties is part of your daily life as a business owner, and unfortunately, it can distract you from what you should be doing because a lot of emotions are at stake. Many of my clients, when they are going through difficulties, feel like someone is poking a knife in their heart. It's their business, their baby, and they fail to understand why someone would treat it that way.

The fact is, if everything was running smoothly without difficulties, you would grow your business without much effort. However, dealing with human emotions from staff to clients makes that simply impossible. We have to accept that their reality is never going to be the same as ours, and it's normal for them to come to work with different agendas. That's why I believe that working on your soft skills of leadership is so important, so you can be flexible enough and keep your mindset strong to overcome everything you are dealing with. The past two years have been a classic example of our energies being tested through adversity.

So, how do we manage difficulties? What can make us more focused? Do we have answers to all of the issues we encounter?

Business needs is the door

Staff morale is the lock

Ethos is the key

Pardon the analogy; it came out as I was writing this. However, I believe that our ethos brings integrity to the business, and without that, it will be difficult to make decisions that suit your business and the demands of your staff.

I have countless examples of difficult situations I had to encounter in my 30-year career, and what seemed impossible once upon a time can be different nowadays. So, as an entrepreneur, we have to accept that life and circumstances change. Can you motivate a 20-year-old like you used to? Nowadays? No chance! But you can certainly provide clear guidelines that will guide them in the direction you want.

One thing to remember is that we have a tendency to generalize how we feel. Let me explain.

One day, while at the spa that I mentioned, which had been experiencing a significant decline over the last five years, I was looking at various solutions to create more revenue. I had identified that Sunday trading had potential. We were generating a lot of revenue, and if we focused on Sundays properly, we could take as much revenue as we do on Saturdays. The clients were more relaxed on Sundays since there were no parking restrictions, and the staff was also a lovely team that got along well.

If I opened earlier and closed later, it would add another four hours to the day. If we multiply that by the number of days in a month, it would give us an additional day's trading to the month, which, as far as I was concerned, was a strong opportunity.

So I spoke to my local council, and since it was a small business, all I had to do was pay an extra £120 for the year to change my opening hours. I discussed it with the managers at our weekly meeting and started the process. I had to talk to the team about it (it was always the same team as they had a four-day a week rota, and one team was working Saturdays, and the other on Sundays). I had to ensure that operationally we could follow through with reception and management, and also create a campaign around it so that everyone would take advantage of this. I even created a VIP pass for our strong clients.

I came to work the following day, and the manager on duty said, "Everyone has an issue with it, Valerie. You're going to have a war on your hands. They are far from happy."

Here we go... First, how do they know, I thought. But also, who are "they"?! As mentioned, we have a tendency to put everyone in the same basket, but most of the time, it's just one or two people who stir the pot. When it comes to livelihood, most people will follow to some extent but never wish to lose their job. If they all do at once, then you do have a problem, and you should contact me immediately!

So I turned to her and said, "OK, who are they? You're going to phone everyone who is one day off or on holiday. You're going to speak to everyone on duty, and I want names of the people who are unhappy about this so I can speak to them. But most of all, let me deal with the manager whom I knew had opened his big mouth. He never did that again, I can tell you that for sure! Gossiping is counterproductive.

Commitment from my managers was absolutely crucial. Since I never had the opportunity to launch this initiative properly, I needed to give him a piece of my mind, as now I do have a war on my hand. You see, I would always bring a "bad subject" on an individual basis, never in a group or in a gossipy manner.

Anyhow, she came back… out of 50 people in the team, five had an issue. Out of the five I spoke to and explained (again, on an individual basis) why I was doing this, as people always like to know why they do what you want them to do. It's never justifying yourself, although it can feel like it, but it's finding common ground to a solution and applying it together. Only one had a true issue and became so difficult, I had to deal with her in a different manner… Guess what? She was never on shift on Sundays! She was only working Saturdays… She simply needed to have her say, stir the issues and put her 2 pence worth. Power to the people: "we never did that before" kind of attitude.

Roll drum to Flossy... So this Flossy is what makes your challenges and I have identified some to name a few: from the moody to the scatty, from the plain rude to the queen of the castle, from the annoying chatterbox to the opinionated, from the plain vicious to the unbearable, from the backstabber to the sarcastic... and the list goes on... I am sure you have identified someone in your mind.

I have learned that throughout the years, reacting gets you nowhere but sets a tone and is never positive for the outcome. When I explained that I would put this on trial for three months and if it didn't work, would revert back to the normal hours, when I suggested that we would open three hours instead of four as I understood that Sunday trains are a nightmare so it would be ok to finish at 6pm instead of the 7pm originally thought of, when I calculated their extra commission and put an incentive in place, the team was ok, although skeptical, to trial it, as they too understood we needed to bring this place up. It was a success, we stayed like this forever and everyone was happy.... Apart from my biggest Flossy of all who tried to create her own mini-revolution and failed, as I was standing up to my ethos and procedures for misbehavior. She did go on disciplinary, she never left, and we tolerated each other in the end.

There are so many different situations and characters we deal with on a day to day basis that can be classified as difficult and these are the effects of having to deal with a difficult situation or team member:

1. It can take up a lot of your energy. I felt drained for days on end from these tricky situations.

2. You can learn a great deal from each situation but there can be a lot of negatives before you see the positives. Some situations can take years to get over.

3. It can be hard to find a solution and it is not easy to know who you should turn to.

4. It can be time consuming and take up much of your concentration.

5. Difficult staff members can be disruptive to the other staff in your business. They have a tendency to become the focal point of the business.

In other words, they want attention.

As a manager/owner, we deal with negative situations constantly, and we are often in the midst of it all. Ironically, in our industry, we are responsible for promoting wellbeing and taking care of people, but difficult team members can sap any notion of wellbeing. How many times have I heard statements like "If she wasn't there" or "When that stops"?

The first thing you must do is label the situation as a 'Challenging Team Member'. By labeling it in this way, you are removing yourself emotionally from the situation. 'Difficult' is far too negative of a descriptor.

You have dealt with challenges before, and you can get stuck in and not let it affect you. Everything is surmountable. Once you've done that, give your challenge a name: Challenge Christmas, Challenge Nails Crisis, Challenge Holiday Time. By not using the first name of the troublesome individual, you can disassociate yourself from that person. They are a case, a challenge that you are dealing with and sorting out.

The psychology of this is important because we know how difficult team members can occupy our thoughts far too much.

Having given your Challenge a name, answer these four key points and write them down:

→ ASSESSMENT: What is the challenge?

→ CREATE: What should I have in place? What is the source of the issue? What can I do to create best practice? We need to remember that each situation is unique and we can learn from them. We are not always right - challengers are great at telling us this!

➜ DELIVER: How can I reach an amicable solution ? How can I resolve it?

➜ MAINTAIN: What is in place in order to maintain this solution so it doesn't happen again?

Once you have answered these questions, there is only one step left to take: COMMUNICATE.

Communication is key to diffusing difficult situations. It is vital to iron things out and create a verbal contract with all problems. Without communication, assumptions are made and assumptions can be dangerous. Remember it is an industry made by people for people and communication is the only way to resolve and move forward. At this stage, I should call it CONSTRUCTIVE COMMUNICATION.

Creating your best practice folder (Standard Operating Procedure Manual - more on this later) is also key to smooth communication, but usually a long process, so don't wait for this to be completed before you tackle the challenge. However, when the coast is clear, make sure you get this best practice folder completed. Stop delaying it.

In order to communicate with your challenge, you must make time for MEETINGS.

Now, I know it sounds obvious and I am far from reinventing the wheel here, however, you will be amazed at how many of us avoid making time for meetings. The key element here is to communicate effectively; you must tackle the challenge head-on.

You must make space in your diary and prioritize such meetings. For four weeks, I would make that challenger see me once a week. Talk, discuss, hear their point of view, and make sure they hear mine. Your angle should be "yes, I understand your point of view, but for the business, this is what I need." It is advisable to take a positive approach.

A business owner challenged me on this and mentioned that if she had done this to her challenge, she would have said, "you are picking on me" and would limit bullying. Of course, you must adapt this to your challenge and create a solution for each of them.

The question is: How often are you holding individual meetings as well as team meetings? You will find that the more regular you are, the more you will be able to iron things out quicker.

ADAPTING AND COMMUNICATING are the keys to successful management of your challenge….

. . .

What are the consequences?

After the month has passed with your weekly meetings and things have improved, you may choose to let it go. Have they understood what you are doing? Has the atmosphere improved? Are the required standards being met? If this is the case, then you can put them on Performance Management. These will be official meetings where you will take notes and make them sign them. You can decide how long you want to give them time for improvement, up to three months to really give them a chance to improve. You should ensure that communication is still positive and encouraging, and set the tone of support. There are three ways this can go:

1. They will either carry on with their behavior.

2. They will understand, and you will reach an amicable solution.

3. They will resign.

Performance Management has a tendency to set the tone, and they rarely want to go to the next step.

Now, it doesn't mean that they will hear you, listen to you, or even respect you. Sometimes the response will be defensive. However, by just installing that communication process, you are taking control while also giving the employee the attention they are craving.

If the behavior still continues, then you will need to go through a disciplinary procedure.

Disciplinary Procedures:

There are amazing websites you can use or you can go to your solicitor. Going through a legal procedure will affect the relationship and will have consequences but can be beneficial for all in the end.

Before you are going down that route, I have created the 123 chat method® which gives someone three chances or warnings. I tell you once, nicely, I tell you twice, a little more firm and the third time you are going on disciplinary. With a clear method, you are setting boundaries. Some would argue that we need to be more flexible since we are finding it hard to recruit, however, if you have a lack of systems in place then it will be a free for all and your leadership will be less than empowering. Now your flexibility will oversee anything on a case by case basis but if the same thing happens and there are zero consequences, it will go against you

. . .

→ ISOLATE

The challenger is the one to isolate. Use language such as: "You are the only one thinking that way - no one else thinks that." The more isolated they feel, the less power they have. Reiterate and follow up the others to get them on your side sort of speak.

→ REASSESS

Stop brushing things under the carpet; revisit the issues every now then, be in control and happy with your decisions. You want this challenger to feel that nothing gets to you. You are approachable in the way you manage situations but everything comes down to the business needs.

On a last note, praising good behaviour goes a very long way, regardless of your differences, you must acknowledge when someone does better.

 Sometimes those who challenge you the most teach you the best. - Anonymous

Confession Time!

Marie had a South African therapist who worked for her for over a year. One year in April, she asked Marie for the whole month of December off as she wanted to go back to South Africa. Marie

understood that coming from far away, having just two weeks off was difficult to endure, especially at that time of the year. But she knew that if she gave her the month off, especially at her business's busiest time, she needed to do the same for the others; otherwise, it would become very unfair. Plus, she would be losing too much money with one person down.

She came back with a proposal, having thought about it, and mentioned that she could give her three days off before Christmas and take the four weeks off from then. This would be a one-off in her business. The staff member was upset and became the biggest flossy she ever had to deal with. Marie felt she had given her a solution and was not backing down. Flossy gave her notice early in November, which Mary was expecting and slightly relieved from her bad attitude. It's impossible to win them all! This staff member had the cheek to reapply when she came back from her holiday… Compromise goes both ways. Had both done that, she would still have a job… Marie became a leader here.

6. EMPOWER

Empowerment to me is the key that allows your leadership to flourish. The more each of your staff members can feel empowered to work better and thrive in a constructive environment, the more you are able to work on your business rather than in it, constantly fighting fires everywhere and ultimately become the micromanager from hell without even realizing it.

Every leader will empower their team in their own style, but it will be the consistency in encouraging your team that will drive them towards building their future and ultimately your success for the long run. Their success is your success and vice versa.

What is empowerment of your team looking like?

To me, empowerment goes hand in hand with team culture, which has more of a chance to grow when you have created strong foundations through clear procedures and structure. Hence why I am so operational in the way I function. Once all of the systems are in place, you can focus on your team.

Building a team culture is crucial, and as a leader, taking each personality and making them want to work together in peace and harmony, like an orchestra, you need to become the maestro of your team, and that is pure leadership as far as I am concerned. It is why your team meetings and team building are so important.

Team culture comes in various shapes and forms, but it ultimately comes from the top. A micromanager will find it very difficult to engage in any form of team culture: "They're going to leave anyway," "What's the point, they don't care," "They are never engaged," "No one is as bothered as me."

You name it, the excuses come in bucket loads, the fear of change or even the conviction of their belief becomes overwhelming and stops the growth to some extent. Repetition becomes your best friend when it comes to teams, and your constant drum of ethos and expectations will eventually get through to them. If they still ignore you, you must wonder if that staff member has become a Flossy at some point or another and is dragging the others down with them, because if your team culture is growing, then Flossy should be standing out like a sore thumb. It's time to create a plan of action to deal with your Flossy then.

Ultimately, an empowered team follows their leaders and feels a part of their journey, no matter what happens. A team that finds their leader approachable will have room to grow and input their valuable expertise.

. . .

Why do we need to focus on empowering the team?

→ ACCOUNTABILITY

The main key to any team is giving them enough autonomy for them to feel accountable for their actions and start thinking for themselves. Accountability can be difficult to nurture since it's dependent on the team in front of you. But everything that has been discussed in this book, such as not spoon-feeding information, asking them to come to you with solutions instead of issues, and discussing their numbers, is crucial for them to feel and be more accountable.

Some teams function well without too many layers of management, as they prefer to deal with things themselves, and in some cases, this works well as long as everyone knows what they need to do. Again, procedures and follow-ups should be mega clear.

I believe that accountability is when you, as a leader, stop trying to control every aspect of the business and let them report back to you as to what they need to focus on or do next.

Ultimately, the more expectations you set and the more follow-ups you do with clear and concise feedback, the more likely you are to engage the individuals in front of you. Again, consistency is the key to ensuring that the staff know the direction they ought to take, and caring about what they do so you can guide them to success, ultimately leading to the success of your business. It's a win-win situation.

→ IMPROVED PRODUCTIVITY

Empowering your team automatically improves productivity because they want to be part of your action. When you have an empowered team, it's incredible how much they give back to you because they want to, not because they feel obliged to. I really feel that when they buy into your way of working, it ultimately grows them and allows them to feel part of what you want to achieve. So, when you empower your team, as far as I am concerned, you are automatically improving their productivity. A happy team equals happy customers, and happy customers mean happy cashflow for the long run.

→ THINKING FOR THEMSELVES

When it comes to teams thinking for themselves, it creates an optimum team culture. However, most micromanagers will quickly stamp out this freedom because they refuse to have a different way of working or cannot control what is happening. Even if they encourage it sometimes, they need to know everything at every step of the way so they can input their ways upon them. Is that empowering? I think you know the answer. It is simply the opposite!

When a team starts thinking for themselves, you can feel like a leader who trusts them to get on with it. I want to repeat again and again, if you have clear processes and structures in place, it is easier for them to know your expectations. When the team goes beyond that, you know you have reached a different level.

Once I had a day when I needed to go to head office, called by my boss for something that had to happen immediately. I had to leave my team to get on with an event that we had organized. I called my managers and asked them to go through their action plan for the day. Happy with what they were saying, a tad stressed in how the event was going to run without too many clients confirming, I had to trust the process and the fact that I was unable to attend, knowing full well that if it was going to be a flop my boss would make a comment on it!

Unknown to me, the team ended up calling friends and family to fill up the numbers, gathered their biggest clients and focused their energy on making it a success. When your team has that spirit, you know that you have built a business that is worth every effort, and the result from that event was better than expected. But the numbers achieved were not even the focus. The energy, photos, and togetherness were worth every penny.

The key there is to acknowledge, praise, and thank them. It goes a long way and lifts everyone around you.

How can we empower them?

Have you ever asked each of them about their vision for themselves?

I love getting to know every single one of them and their vision so I can help them achieve it. We are often scared to hear stuff such as "I want to be a business owner and open my own salon" or "I want to be an actor one day!" Of course, it's never easy for you as a business owner to not understand why they wouldn't want to stay with you forever since you have built your own baby.

Although you know that leaders build leaders, the thought of them leaving you one day and having to start all over, trusting someone, and restarting again can fill you with dread. However, the minute you stop attaching importance to the outcome, the moment you find that all of this becomes bearable. "I have them for as long as they want to stay with me, let me make the most of them while they are here" was always my first thought process.

When you buy into their own dreams and aspirations, you find that they feel more at ease with you and your business. There are fewer sneakiness and hidden agendas when everything is out in the open. One of my hairstylists wanted to be an actor, so I made a deal with him that if he met his target in four days a week instead of five, he could still earn his money and have an extra day off during the day for his acting coach. We agreed on a three-month trial, which was very successful. He was motivated to do overtime to reach his goal in four days, so much so that he stayed with me longer than anticipated as he compensated for his one day off by upselling, cross-selling, and retailing like crazy. If you can generate a win-win situation with your staff members, you will find that it will bring in more productivity and happiness all around.

On the other hand, I just spoke to an owner who has to reduce hours for her team as the business needs to survive a difficult transition. One of the managers who was already underperforming started to negotiate her hours and when it would suit her. Moreover, this manager is never upselling, cross-selling, or retailing, which leads to a lack of engagement with her clientele for the business to grow. How long can you accept that behavior, especially when you are struggling as an owner? I stood firm in what was needed in the business and told her there are zero negotiations to be had; it is what it is, and that's that. You're not pleasing people for a better outcome. You empower them to want to do better, that's the difference between leading and managing a situation. You may be afraid to change, but it can be more beneficial for you, especially when it comes to the survival of the business.

→ OPEN AND HONEST COMMUNICATION

I believe that open communication is the only way to grow yourself and everyone else around you. I have listened to meetings where the owner is putting their opinion on everything and, therefore, never allowing for "freedom of speech".

Let me give you an example here: The owner had an issue with a lazy employee, Flossy, and had a meeting with her. Instead of listening to her staff member and why she was being lazy, the owner was just stating what she felt. Every sentence implied something, as there were too many closed questions, which gave the staff member little room to express themselves. When the staff member managed to put her point across, it was shut down very quickly with far too many assumptions:

Building Trust

"You never have done it this way because you dislike it, don't you?" "You did this because you were far from being bothered, didn't you?"

Okay, then. That's what you believe. That's what happened. Maybe with a passive-aggressive approach, there is very little room for your employee to grow and exchange. Of course, there are plenty of occasions where you need to be firmer, in which case, there should be more direct communication. Respect is earned, and the team can hear you if you are more consistent in your approach.

Trying to find out why they are doing it this way is far more beneficial: "Tell me, why are you doing it this way? How do you think this will affect the reception team?" You are encouraging a conversation and understanding their thought process. Plus, they might have a point you never thought of, so active listening is mega important, as mentioned before. In the case of that salon owner, the staff member had a point. Reception was very inconsistent in their support. The staff member was confused, and although I suspect she was a little lazy, she had some points that needed to be considered for an overall better atmosphere.

I find that once the communication is more empowering, you will end up creating a constructive feedback culture. I always wanted to know their thought process, so I could reassess and revisit what we did right or what could be improved. As long as the customer journey is affected for the better, I definitely want to have this open and honest feedback mentality. They are the ones working with the customers all the time. Always have that win-win mindset so your team's success is your success and vice versa. Transparency and honesty are always clear communication that works both ways and is a winning combination in my eyes. When an owner is scared of how they will behave if they have too much information, I understand that there are difficult teams out there. It is still key to be transparent on what you can and facilitate that open communication. I am thinking of numbers here; a lot of owners never want to be too transparent on those in case the staff members want to go and work alone. I get that it can be scary to be too open, but there are ways of monitoring their success without having to discuss numbers. However, being open to listening is always strong leadership, and your team will respect you more for it. I have a client whose manager is leaving, and she is struggling to come to terms with it. I told her to speak to each of their staff members and get them on board to support her. That's open communication. Get them to buy into your ups and downs.

I also believe that feedback is important. From you to them and them to you, I reverse the pyramid of communication and encourage the team to give ideas (Idea box in the staff room, anonymously, is brilliant!) The more you think of your staff culture coming from them rather than you, the more you will empower their creativity.

Becoming a leader can be confusing. On one hand, I have to give enough freedom to my team, but on the other, I have to control some form of structure so they know what is expected of them. Again, think win-win: this is how it works here, but we are open to new ideas and energy to make our business even greater. Your actions, however, speak louder than words, which is why your organizational skills, meetings, and focus need to be consistent. Introducing someone new to the team in the right way becomes crucial so that the team welcomes their fresh approach.

➔ ACKNOWLEDGEMENT OF THEIR PROGRESS

Acknowledgment is key to empowering others. Recognizing their progress or work is important, as it may be the most empowering feeling for someone who receives it. Giving someone time to discuss and acknowledge what they have done means a lot and encourages them to receive more feedback and do better each time.

To this day, I still write down everything that I need to acknowledge, from clients to connections or work colleagues. It is always been a part of my ethos to take that time. I believe that it is the key to being remembered as a leader, as everyone around you will believe that you care. And that in itself goes a long way. Beyond pay increases, acknowledgment is the most impactful empowerment of them all.

Alongside acknowledgment of their progress, recognition and appreciation of their input are even stronger indicators of their importance in your business. The more you do that, the more you will receive from them.

➜ ALLOWING MISTAKES

This can be difficult for micromanagers as they often feel they don't have time for mistakes, and their mindset becomes "I would rather do it myself". Allowing for mistakes to happen is the only way for employees to learn. I always ask myself whether I have communicated effectively, but ultimately, I want to ensure that I have followed up in an efficient manner rather than sporadically.

"What can you learn from your mistakes? How can you do better next time? Have you thought of a way to improve?" These questions are key to empowering staff members to do better each time. Over the years, I have found that giving tasks that are relevant to what employees want to do is essential to their development and ultimate empowerment.

When it comes to empowerment, it is important to avoid being "too nice" as you may be taken advantage of. I am always firm but fair, and I know some people loved working with me while others avoided me like the plague. I don't mind because I want people to want to work with me rather than feeling forced into a culture they are not engaged in.

I can hear you thinking, "But I will have no one in my team if I carry on like that!" It is better to have a smaller team that is engaged in your business than a larger team that just exists without any engagement. However, it is important to remember that every team is different and every leader is different. Ultimately, your success should be based on whether you are happy with the outcome, revenue, and direction of the business, or if you are constantly frustrated.

Learning leadership will constantly drive you towards incredible growth, and to keep doing so, you need to constantly grow and engage your team to grow with you.

7. LOYALTY

When it comes to loyalty, I feel that we need to discuss the fact that loyalty comes in two ways.

From the employer's perspective:

➜ Being loyal to your business for a long time can be both positive and negative. On one hand, having a team that has been with you for a long time means they are connected to your business, but on the other hand, they can become too relaxed and develop bad habits. This can hinder your business's ability to achieve more and become too comfortable. This is what I call Generation "Brick Wall." They have an "I know what I am doing" attitude and resist change.

I once met an owner with four staff members who had been there for over 20 years each. The business was underperforming to the point where the owner had to borrow money to make ends meet. After analyzing the staff's performance, we discovered that they were uninterested in the changes we needed to implement.

In this case, loyalty had become a negative. We couldn't go in guns blazing and address the behavior immediately after so many years of neglect, so we had to come up with a change management strategy.

We implemented changes in treatment and set targets to emphasize their importance. We also looked at changes in the rota to increase revenue and focused on new clients to monitor success. The changes were small but enough to put a little pressure on the staff to buy into them. We then implemented the 123 method chat® for underperformers.

We also created a strong structure and employed a manager to implement day-to-day tasks. In the end, the two uninterested staff members left on their own accord, and the remaining two showed renewed energy and began performing better. They were finally given the attention they needed to flourish without the underlying negativity from the previous staff members.

➔ On the other hand, loyalty can come in the form of buying into the business and its culture, no matter how long. I used to think that if my new staff member would stay with me for two years, I would be happy. This meant that while they were with me, I would do everything in my power to ensure they were empowered and learned as much as possible. I always set them up for success and having a two-year plan per person was the key to my success with them. More often than not, they would stay longer as I engaged them for the long run.

→ Then there is the clash with the younger generation, which is becoming increasingly important in light of the recruitment crisis we are facing, and that is managing the Generation Z or post-pandemic mindset of wanting to work less and less.

The Generation Theory states that every generation is built in opposition to the previous generation. I mean, what we are going through at the moment is not new! The "It was better before" syndrome is a constant feeling that generates a strong sense of unfairness. But what I really want to emphasize is the fact that this is not new, and we have to be able to adapt as leaders to what is going on with the lack of CVs/resumés and work ethics, just look at the lack of good CVs/resumés! Of course, the pandemic has caused a huge shift in people's mindsets, but there are some wonderful people out there who are great to work with.

It is so important to start emphasizing what works rather than focusing on what is negative. In a webinar that Tiphaine Modeste and I created to discuss this topic, we had identified characteristics of the latest generations:

Baby-boomers (1943 – 1959)	Generation X (1960 - 1977)	Generation Y (1978 - 1994)	Generation Z (1995 - 2009)
Career	Less jobs available	Against authority	Flexible
Respect	Looking for balance	Want balance	Evolution
Loyalty	Less loyalty	Looking for a mentor	Wellness
Feeling you belong	Value of their skills	Independence	Social link
		Team spirit	Want to be taught
			Entrepreneur

From a management's perspective:

→ Spoilt generation

→ Not motivated

→ Not patient

→ Difficult

→ High turnover

→ Lack of motivation and goals

→ Disengaged

→ Difficult to recruit

→ Repeat myself

→ Feeling powerless

From the new generation's perspective:

→ The because before the why

→ Flexibility before security

→ Wellness before success

→ Looking for a coach, mentor

→ Value their skills

→ Hates too much of a routine

→ Want challenges without it being too hard work

→ Wants variety of work

→ Happy at work is key to them

As far as I can see, they have everything at the tip of their fingers, so their values are a lot more defined. I am often shocked at how their wellness comes before anything else, and sometimes feel that this generation wants to have their cake and eat it too. In a way, why not? With everything that is going on in the world, why would you want to work harder than you should? I get that. I can see my two daughters, with a strong work ethic that I have instilled in them from a very young age. Being a single mom generated a value around money that was important for them to have: "You want trainers? You have to work for it!" But I sometimes feel that this generation is never prepared to work as hard as they should to get what they want.

Ultimately, if someone has created a business, the chances are that they have worked extremely hard for it to be successful. So, that's where the generation clashes. They are constantly showing me that there is more to life than work, and that it should be that way. It's normal in the world we live in. We should enjoy every moment of it. It all depends on what you want to achieve, and ultimately working smarter is more and more important. You can become an entrepreneur online at ten, so why think like us oldies? I would say here to avoid putting everyone in one basket.

In an operational business, it's so difficult to foresee how these generations are going to be the future. Maybe that's why robots will take over, but until that's done, until we are embracing a different way of life and adapt to the crush everyone is talking about, I strongly believe that we can carry on building leaders in their own rights. You have the experience and expertise in building your business. You have skills that are beyond what anyone can learn, and no one can take that away from you. Teaching those skills to empower the new generation to me is the most valuable gift of them all.

There are four key aspects of the new generations that are key for them. In a nutshell, this is very much what they are looking for:

1. MEANING TO THEIR ROLE WITH YOU

→ They need to understand where you are going and decide if they want to follow you. Chances are, they can search online for everything about you so being clear in your message, ethos and values will only engage them further.

→ Why do I wake up in the morning? Give them a reason to belong to your business and their valuable input in what you want them to deliver.

→ Define your direction as a business and communicate, whichever the generation. This is key to the transparency you need to adopt as a business owner.

→ Explain why and set expectation. I always feel you need to justify yourself but it's beyond that; people and the new generation, even more, need to understand why it is the task needs to be done. They are more than likely going to appreciate the task itself.

2. TRUST THEIR INPUT

→ They are not here for life and the more you connect with that, the less frustrated you will feel, so empowering them to grow will give them valuable skills for the future, and let's remember that they are your future!

→ Give and Take is always a win-win as far as I can see and we have to be more and more flexible in the way we function as a leader

→ Experiences: let them miss you when they leave and learn that you were the best boss they have ever had, that's leaving a legacy in itself!

→ Skills are developed and sometimes the frustration is that they want to learn everything quickly without trusting the process. The clearer you are in your staff journey, the more consistent you are in developing them, the more they will follow you. How many pearls have I met stuck in a job where the owner simply is never going to build their skills - such a waste and if you can lead those forward, you will have an engagement for life.

→ Development – personal & professional is so key, I am thinking of mental health here that can be very much present at the moment so supporting them in this way can very much have a great influence for them on a professional and personal level.

→ Break the routine: Challenges and games, team-building, different treatment, new training etc.

3. BUILD THEIR KNOWLEDGE

→ Stop thinking that employees are indebted to the company. This can be difficult for you as an owner, especially if they leave to start their own business. However, if you have worked on all aspects of your business and are sure of who you are, nothing will shake its foundation. You can still attract strong teams to your business.

→ Show genuine interest in your employees. The new generation loves to feel valued and loved. If they feel valued, they will be more committed to you than you think.

→ Being a team player is a secretly wonderful feeling for the new generation. Nurture them to become future leaders.

→ Cooperation is key. Break down expectations into small chunks, communicate clearly, and avoid generalizing about the new generation. Focus on the amazing young talents out there, and avoid spreading negativity about the industry.

4. TRANSPARANCY

→ Keep your promises is perhaps most important as they will be disengaged very quickly and suss you out if you keep promising but under-deliver.

→ Recognise your weaknesses is so much better than pretending as, again, they can smell it a mile off - transparency becomes your best friend when managing this younger generation.

→ Adopt different style of leadership to connect with them on another level.

→ Inspire with empathy and support is the key to empower them.

In summary, the employer's perspective is to empower a diverse set of individuals to keep them loyal to their business. But ultimately, being true to oneself as a leader and reevaluating the company's ethos is what will make them the strongest leader. This is because they will attract people who want to work with them and build their dream together. By navigating the ups and downs of the business with a team that wants to follow them, they will be able to achieve success.

From the employee's perspective:

Loyalty means different things to different people but this is what I currently see which makes a difference between a business who has a high staff turnover and one who is more stable:

→ ACKNOWLEDGEMENT: I want to emphasize again the importance of acknowledging employees' progress or when they have done something well. Never underestimate what those words can do for their mindset, and deep, sincere appreciation for their work can go a long way.

→ PRAISE: Praising employees is also an essential aspect of leadership. Always praise them for various things you can see in your business, no matter how small they are. From the cleaner to the managers, every role is important in the well-oiled machine. Never be too busy to appreciate the small details.

→ MONEY: A yearly raise should be part of your ethos and should be dependent on performance. In big corporations, I was guaranteed a 3% raise and up to 5% depending on my performance. This is a way to appreciate your employees' work in your business, and if you stay on top of your numbers, there is always a possibility to adopt this mentality. Ultimately, we work for the love of it, but being acknowledged financially can have an effect on employees' loyalty to you and your business. Reviewing commissions can also be beneficial to ensure it's a win-win situation for both the employee and the business.

→ ENERGY: When you work in a business with the right energy and consistent atmosphere, you are more likely to stay there. I am thinking of my daughter's current jobs, which may not be lifelong roles, but the positive energy they feel in those roles outweighs any flaws that could be improved upon. One of them even said that it's so nice, she wants to come back to it after traveling. This entrepreneur has completely understood this generation, treats them well, and remains flexible in meeting their wants and needs. They keep coming back to him because the energy, pay, and atmosphere are relaxed yet focused at the same time. It's a great example of how a workforce can be loyal to a business without being forced. Although they are very procedure-driven (it's a Patisserie, so they have to be) and strict in some ways, the way they respect each employee and their values makes it a great business to belong to. It can be challenging to think like this and apply it when you're serving people, but stop putting expectations on the outcome, as it can constantly disappoint you.

→ STABILITY: This can be difficult during challenging times, especially when a recession looms for future years or decades. However, customers and staff are looking for a stable business. The ones that invest in newness and keep growing despite all the challenges. Employees feel safe when they don't see their employer stressed all the time, which generates a stronger business foundation.

Structure

Your structure is everything. And I mean everything. Even if your business is small, you always have solutions to delegate and outsource, which we will see in the other chapters.

I believe that if your structure is working against you, then you will end up in micromanagement and be stuck on that constant wheel. It is crucial that your structure becomes an integral part of your business so everything is clear: who is who and who does what.

This way, you can stop micromanagement and focus on what you should be focusing on. As far as I am concerned, your structure is the key to leadership and will stop micromanagement as the systems that follow that structure will enable everyone to flourish, including you and your work-life balance.

It can be difficult to invest in a structure when we are in the depth of a recession and everything is uncertain, but the more you focus on lack, the more your business will reflect that, and the more it will fall all on you as an owner, hence why I have seen a rise in micromanagement. Ultimately, it's all down to your budget and forecast which can allow you to grow in a strategic way. It will also send a message to your team and customers alike that you are strong and will do everything for everyone to be able to do their role to the best of their abilities, and that in itself generates loyalty and stability.

Create your Organigram with as much information as you can, even contact details if you wish, so you can use this for your new welcome pack for new starters. It can look like this:

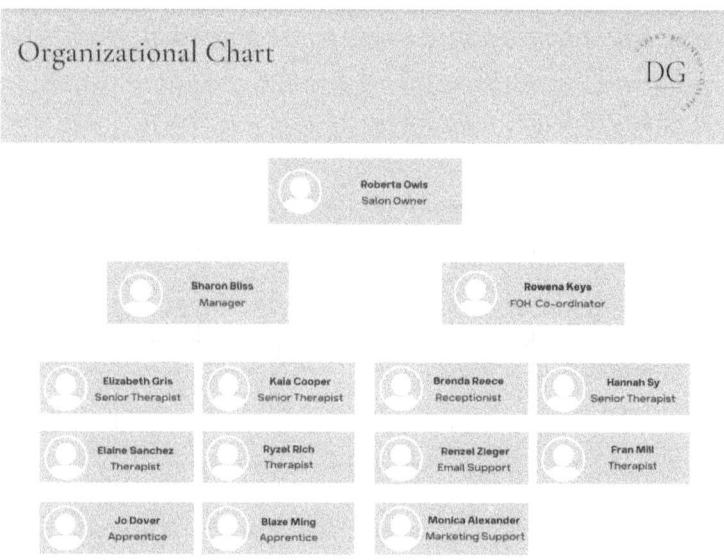

Once you have defined the Organigram, create a list of who does what in the business - this is also fantastic to add to the new welcome pack so all is clear but also definitely keep a list in your operating manual.

The clearer you are in your structure, the clearer will be the team and ultimately it will impact the customer journey.

A great exercise is to separate your teams into three groups and ask:

One group to write down what the owners and managers does

One group to write down what the reception does

One group to write down what the service provider does.

(You can amend that to your industry)

Give them ten minutes to discuss among themselves, and then have each group stand up and discuss their findings with the others. It's a great way to understand each other's roles and become more flexible in the way they think. If everyone does what they're supposed to do, you'll have a smoothly running business!

I also loved to pair up employees from different departments during quiet times so they could understand each other's roles. It's a fantastic way to gain respect within each department.

Standard Operating Procedure (SOP) Manual

If a client journey is essential to consolidate customer service and elevate standards within your business, so is a Standard Operating Procedures manual. In fact, every business that employs staff should have an SOP manual (Standard Operating Procedure manual), but many businesses never understand why and where to start when it comes to writing it. The manual also helps you manage staff and is an excellent tool in setting up expectations for you and your team. Whatever is in your head is on paper.

Learn everything you need to know to plan the writing of your manual efficiently. If you do have one, when was the last time it was updated? How often do you use it?

What Exactly Is This Handbook?

By definition, this manual contains every single procedure, each written as detailed as possible.

. . .

Why Is This Manual So Important?

Procedures are essential to ensure a smooth running of the business. This procedure manual helps maintain standards across your business. Should you ever wish to expand your venture and manage staff correctly, everything that you want to happen in your business is written down.

A folder with all your operation procedures guarantees that when you're away, your colleagues/employees can find everything they need to know if a situation they were unfamiliar with arises.

SOP Manuals Unify Customer Service & Experience

An essential aspect of this guide is that it unifies the ways your employees react to certain situations within your business.

Create and review your business procedures as you go: What suppliers do you have, and when was the last time you checked if you can find better business agreements? What is the current recruitment procedure? Can you implement a form of telephone interview? Where do you find the most efficient, cost-effective locksmith? What is your laundry procedure?

What are your Health and Safety procedures? Have you got all your protocols listed? The list goes on.

Where Should It Be Found?

Keep your manual on your desk. Think of it as a "live" folder with your business's operational best practices; something everyone can (and should) refer to. By having it close by at all times, it's easier to make any amendments or updates, should you have any to do.

Who Can Access It?

Everyone! There are no secrets in your procedures; in fact, you should encourage your team to look at and update the folder themselves when necessary! For newcomers, why not get them to read through it as part of their induction?

However, bear in mind that this folder shouldn't be taken out of your business. It is your intellectual property. You don't want someone to copy everything and create their own business with your SOP!

When Do I Start?

Now! There is no time like the present to start listing your operational procedures. You have most of it already; it just needs to be written down and put together. The more detailed you are, the better you can guide your team(s) to act upon your standards.

How Long Will It Take?

From scratch, it will take as long as you need to finalize everything. Since you are working in between, it can take you a year before you have everything under one roof and make it your own. Start by listing what you need to include in your guide and assess when you can realistically create your manual. Create deadlines for yourself for every section and stick to them. Make sure you think of what is essential for your business first.

Writing your SOP manual may seem daunting at first, but in reality, it's not that hard. You have most of your procedures in mind; it's just about writing them down for your team to be able to rely on them.

Implementation:

It's all well and good to have your procedures, but if there are no consequences for their actions or non-actions, then you may as well not bother. Make it part of your team training, have it implemented as part of your individual meetings, or welcoming to new staff.

We provide a framework for you to start your own SOP here at The Delforge Group®.

Outsourcing

When looking at your workload and determining who does what, it's important to remember that you can outsource certain tasks to other experts. You can outsource a virtual personal assistant, administrative support, or even cleaning services to offload big cleaning jobs that you have to do on a Sunday. Simply create a list of tasks that are taking up too much of your time and that you would rather not do, and then start creating an action plan of who could do what, from your team to your family members.

Outsourcing can be cost- and time-effective, and it's something that I review every single year. I ask myself if my time is being well-spent and if the money I'm spending is being used efficiently, or if it could be better spent elsewhere. The more you focus on your to-do list and your workload, the more time you'll have to let your leadership skills flourish.

Letting Go of the Past

Letting go of how you function can be the most difficult of them all. Letting go of what you know and moving forward to a different way of working and being can be both scary but, most of all, rewarding. It is the inner structure of change that starts with your flexibility of mind and overcoming all of the challenges that ultimately creates a strong way of functioning for your future.

In order for you to be able to let go of the past, start by revisiting the way things are done and all of the systems in place: are they serving you or are they working against you?

I strongly believe that it's when you get the team to buy into what you want to achieve by asking for feedback that you can successfully let go of the old ways. It's so important that you revisit the goals of the business, the systems in place and make sure that everyone is aligned with the vision of the company. Encourage open communication and let your team know that their input is valuable.

Remember that change takes time, so be patient with yourself and your team. Celebrate small wins and keep pushing forward towards the bigger picture.

→ A fresh pair of eyes: from a new staff member to a coach, from a mystery shop to you visiting your own business with the client's hat, it's always great to get feedback and embrace a new way of doing things. Sometimes we are too busy running around we forget the essentials, and in order to grow, you must be open to constructive criticism, which will allow you to understand a different perspective. I used to sit in the reception area and observe, pretending I was writing. It's fascinating as they forget you are there.

→ Simply listen to new people in your organization: the emphasis is on communication here, and active listening, which, I am unsure if you have noticed, but keeps coming back here! Encouraging feedback and listening to what is being said is the most powerful tool you can have within your business. Being open to change is then down to you. I find that change management can take time; it's all the small changes that you will create that will make a big difference in the end.

→ Step away from the vision for a minute: if you are feeling overwhelmed and uncertain about your direction, stop for a moment and reassess. We are constantly talking to our members about securing some time out of the business quarterly to reassess where they are at. It gives you the freedom and focus you need to oversee what is happening in the business. Listening to your gut can sometimes only be done if you are stopping and allowing yourself that time out. If you are really unable to do so, then sit in your business with a different hat for a moment. Go back to the shop floor at reception or cutting hair, whichever it may be. It might give you a different perspective of what is truly happening in your business.

→ The newness that wants to be born, we get to know that it's for us if we listen or pay attention. This will be down to the operation in place so you can begin to flourish as a business. We see it with rotating spaces or displays when you change them around (and we do suggest you do that quarterly). Suddenly the client sees something different. I remember when I moved the body products to the front as it was the season to highlight them, customers were saying they never knew we did body products. They had been on the shop floor for ten years at the back! If clients can notice changes as small as these, you can too if you pay attention. That newness can also be brought in through the employees, especially the new ones, so encourage that rather than being closed to comments and the mindset of "we have always done it this way." When you are open and available to change, you allow for success to happen collectively, and that is true leadership.

. . .

Flourishing is more important than thriving. Practicing something that is greater than yourself with the mindset of "we can expand from it" becomes a way of being, rather than just a way of working. I believe that creating a strong approach to leading your business spills over into your personal life, allowing you to grow as an overall leader of your life. This, in turn, allows you to become more well-rounded in your approach, less critical, and less focused on perfection. To me, this is the ultimate approach for a leader because you end up flourishing in both your personal and professional life.

6
SEEING THE BIGGER PICTURE

A Clear Vision

A clear vision can help drive your business forward and support your growth, but most importantly, it can empower others as they understand where you're taking the business. The clearer the vision, the clearer the message to everyone around you, including staff and customers. When you wake up with that tingling feeling of knowing where you're driving the business towards, you smile towards the bright future ahead of you. It's that gut feeling that propels you towards your dream defined by your vision and mission.

However, it's easy to lose sight of the vision when day-to-day operations consume your focus. Being an electrician, therapist to your team, and juggling your work/life balance can be overwhelming, and the vision can be lost year after year or simply forgotten. We offer programs to help define your vision and create quarterly missions to achieve it. Quarterly focuses are flexible and provide ample time to achieve missions, empowering you to achieve even more.

We've found that the pressure of keeping your business afloat, recruiting staff with their own intentions, and navigating the current state of the world can be demotivating. In a recent workshop, Amy shared that she includes her dream car in her yearly vision, but she hasn't seen it parked in front of her house for the past five years. How can she believe in it? Writing it down has become a habit, but it's not yet a reality or a feeling that makes her jump out of bed with excitement.

It can be challenging to envision a future that feels uncertain in a world full of madness and constant bad news.

I believe that there is intense pressure for a lot of people to lead the "social media life". Unless you have everything sorted and are perfect in every aspect of your life, you can feel like a failure. Having had two daughters, I understand that this pressure is very real. In business, this pressure to be perfect can increase our micromanagement tendencies because we want to control every aspect of it, and as we know, this only increases the intensity of the best outcome.

If you take the pressure off controlling the outcome, you can only do your best to try and achieve it, which releases the need for everything to be perfect. For example, having a fancy car was the outcome of earning more money through understanding his numbers and creating a budget. How about we look at creating a budget, knowing how much we need and for how long we would need to save to eventually get the car? By being more practical and realistic in his monthly focus, the vision becomes clearer. His vision for the next year would be to be on top of his expenditure and budget. Let's work on that for one year, revisit it, and keep focusing on it. Chances are that the outcome might even be better, and he might even be able to buy a top-end car by really focusing, or he might have changed his mind and wanted a different car by then, but the process still got him there. What you put your mind to can become a reality if you want it hard enough. Small steps, remember, make a giant one in the end.

So, if we avoid writing a vision that is too big and feels too unrealistic according to our situation, let's stop that right now. We have been talking a lot about ditching the vision because it adds to the pressure that you might already feel. However, there is something that works and has worked for me every single year. Being a single mum, most of the time, I was grateful for finishing the year with all the chaos that motherhood and work brought to me. So I always had a vision for the year ahead: what do I want to achieve by the end of next year, on a personal and professional level? Write it down, dissect it into quarterly missions, and that makes it far more achievable and real. It allows me to feel that sense of achievement and pride. Some years I would achieve more than expected, some years less, but I was flexible enough to overcome those challenges.

I write the quarterly missions in my planner and diary so that I have it at hand at all times and ensure I take one day every quarter to revisit where I am with it all. Take a B&B, hotel lobby, or happy place, one day, three days, a week, whatever feels good to your soul, but take that time. Recenter and refresh yourself from the busy times. It's so important.

Now, working with various people, I have encountered some incredible visionaries who multiply their vision by ten: they want a house and multiply it by ten so it becomes a ranch, they want a car and multiply it by ten so it becomes a top-of-the-range car, etc. If that works for you and you can visualize it, then go for it! It's amazing!

For me, it never spoke to me as I found it all too unrealistic. But after watching The Secret, listening to powerful podcasts, reading Napoleon Hill's Think and Grow Rich, and all of the great influencers of the subconscious mind to make your reality, I have found that meditating and journaling works for me. It makes me feel complete and calm about my future. I love gratefulness and have achieved beyond my expectations. I am simply content, and that is plenty for me. My aim has always been to support as many people as I can. I have so much empathy, so my sense of achievement is fulfilled.

But whatever you want, whatever you desire, you can achieve it. It takes working at your own pace, your own peace. There is never a right or wrong way of doing things; there is simply your way, and that is good enough. Stop listening to too many things and listen to your gut. Do what makes you satisfied and complete, but do it with an understanding that you can achieve whatever you set out to.

In your life, once you have set up your systems, make them work for you rather than against you so that you have time to keep growing in your plan and working on your mindset.

A clear vision, whether it is a huge one or a yearly one, will empower you and everyone else around you. My sister once told me, "You are like the light of a candle. If it's flickering, everything else around you will be. If it's stable and strong, everything around you will shine brightly." Keep shining and keep focused. No matter what happens to you, be flexible enough to work around it, surround yourself with systems and processes that make your life easier, but overcome it through the vision that you have.

And that to me is true leadership. Whatever you feel, you should know one thing: How do I visualize myself for the year ahead? What does that look like?

Unlock the Blockages

It is difficult to even know if we have blockages. Most of the time, micromanagers are focusing on their own way of working and nothing else can work better than their ways. So, what blockages? But if you are on the path of change, this is an important aspect of your growth. This inner change will automatically have an effect on every single aspect of your life.

To me, there are a few aspects of unblocking your blocks, whether it be money, fear, managing people, or even self-belief. No matter the barrier, these must be worked on:

1. Create healthy habits that work for you.

2. Comparison is the thief of joy, you must focus on your own path.

3. Find what drives you and focus on that.

4. Get support, whether it be a coach, a therapist, a sport, or a supportive friend. Find what makes you feel good and supports your growth.

5. Think about what you want life to look like and maintain your focus.

6. Learn about your soft skills and focus on the one you believe will support your growth. Resilience, for example, is a strong leadership skill at this stage that will allow your growth.

7. Self-discipline starts within, even one small change can make you feel a lot better.

One of the biggest aspects of growth is committing to your mental health and creating a strong support mechanism to cope with the day-to-day and support in your direction. It is important to invest in what you believe will make you stronger, happier, and create a powerful path to change for the better. I love this quote: "If you don't like where you are, move, you are not a tree."

One problem is that Marc and Marie out there might not even know they have blockages. But having worked and continuing to work with many, I can guarantee you that there is always something in their way of working that they know they need to change. Once they taste the success of change, they are more than likely to open themselves to more of that.

Emotional blocks are an unhealthy relationship with our feelings. We have a hard time understanding what we want, even if we know we want change. Small steps can make a giant difference in the long term.

Since the pandemic, I have been constantly saying one sentence: "Can we calm down!" I feel that the pressure to be perfect and to have it all figured out is so intense that we just need to calm down.

I have always focused on one thing that I knew would help me grow and made it my sole focus for the year ahead, whether it be time management, money mindset, health, leadership, etc. I like to think of one word for the year ahead and makes it my whole focus. My word for 2023 is dedication: dedication to grow my clients' businesses, to empower as many people as I can, and dedication to work on my work-life balance.

Your blockages are normal, human, and it's okay to have them. How about starting to admire your path and what you have achieved and patting yourself on the back? Well done! I am proud of you. And for this year, I am going to work on this aspect of myself to grow.

Being more relaxed in your approach will automatically create a strong focus for you and release the pressure that this social media world is adding upon us. Focus on yourself and your path.

I recently took on a new member who has a lot of work to do to achieve what she wants but keeps doubting herself. One of her clients gave her negative feedback about what she should do in her business. On her second meeting with me, she started saying that she should add a new treatment and look into a new machine to bring newness, and so on.

"And breathe," I said. "Your mental block is that you want to please everyone. Chances are that you will not even see her investing in your new treatment. Everyone has something to say about everything. It's time to trust your process and create habits around your life." I gave her three very clear things to work on before we met again: two professional and one personal to grow her mindset.

Stop distracting yourself with everything and everyone else; it will only divert you from things that can't grow you in a strategic way. Believe in what you can achieve; you have already come so far. Well done. When was the last time you took time out to understand your blockages and work on them in a healthy manner rather than beating yourself up about them?

Keep calm and carry on, that British mindset, has never rung so true when it comes to you and your growth.

Confession Time!

One of Marc's salon managers took the initiative to organize a team meeting in the morning to boost morale and create a strong sense of team gathering. However, when Marc checked his diary with the manager, he questioned everything about the meeting that he just discovered. He wanted a minute-by-minute plan of what was going to happen in the meeting and what was going to be discussed since he was going to be in another meeting with a supplier. The manager, who was keen to have something more fluid and relaxed, ended up feeling rather stressed about it all and cancelled the meeting altogether. He suggested that Marc create it himself when he would have the time. It seems that Marc prefers to do everything himself and control what is being said, rather than giving his managers the lead. When asked, the manager said he was going to do everything in his power to attend the meeting or even watch the camera to see what was happening, so what's the point of cancelling it?

The Systematic Approach

When I worked with Laurent Prieur a few years back and asked him to let me know his thoughts on micromanagement and why it happens. He confirmed what I believe: micromanagement is a psychological pattern focused on control. He suggested I look into the systemic approach to understand the bigger picture. He said, "Where micromanagement is focused on too many details and short horizons, adopting a systemic view of things allows you to take a step back and understand the need to delegate to enable the innovation and agility that your organization needs to adapt to increasingly chaotic variations in its environment."

One of the examples he gave me is of the Cats of Borneo. You can find a video online called 'System Thinking: A Cautionary Tale' which explains how one decision will have many consequences. In the 1950s, the Dayak people of Borneo were suffering from an outbreak of Malaria, so they called the World Health Organization who had a ready-made solution which was to spray DDT (Dichlorodiphenyltrichloroethane, an insecticide used in agriculture) to kill mosquitoes.

The application of DDT to kill mosquitoes carrying malaria had unintended consequences. It also killed parasitic wasps that controlled thatch-eating caterpillars. Without the wasps, the caterpillars multiplied and destroyed the villagers' roofs. The DDT also affected the island's other insects, which were eaten by geckos. The geckos accumulated high levels of DDT, which killed the island's cats that dined on them. With the cats gone, the island's rat population flourished, causing the plague and destruction of grain stores. The World Health

Organization had to parachute cats into Borneo to stabilize the situation.

Systemic leadership and change expert Jennifer Campbell says, "Leadership that focuses on the larger system is about knowing how strengthening the relationships between people is needed to solve problems that are too big and complex for individuals to solve." I realized I already used the systemic approach, and it's fascinating how we never stop learning. Leaders who open their minds to new ways of thinking give themselves a chance to grow, which micromanagers may find hard to do.

I believe it's crucial to look at everything from all angles before forming an opinion or taking action. There are two sides to the systemic approach:

→ The Micromanagers finding it really hard to change anything, otherwise everything will fall apart

→ The systems and communication that are the key to every businesses that will allow you to redefine your structure and make decisions that will complement each other

A systemic mindset will allow you to identify risks and opportunities from where you least expect them. Micromanagement optimizes what already exists, but a systemic approach enables you to build what should replace what is no longer efficient. However, the challenge is that the big picture is too complex for one person alone, no matter how smart they are. You need others, especially your team, to collaborate with and build stronger relationships. The systemic approach inevitably leads to collaboration and strengthens the links between team members.

So, this all got me thinking...

→ The rise of apps in London, particularly for booking hair or beauty appointments at home, has not helped recruitment issues within the industry. Service providers can make a higher commission without the constraints of a salon's demand. However, this opportunity has its downsides, such as unsuitable hours and additional time spent traveling to and from clients' homes, which can be detrimental to the service provider's bottom line. Nevertheless, if demand for the service is high, it can still be a great opportunity.

→ A modern approach to customer loyalty programs goes beyond the traditional "buy five, get one free" model. Cleverly put together memberships that require monthly or yearly payments can be very successful and supportive from the client's perspective. Another option is to create a "friend" program that offers benefits based on a client's total spending for the year.

Find something that resonates with your budget and clients and focus on building your database.

→ Another salon is building a mobile team to compete with the app by servicing a certain mile radius around the area.

→ One salon created the "silent haircut," catering to clients who are shy or prefer not to engage in conversation during their appointments.

→ Another salon employs mothers to work around their childminding schedules, understanding the shortage of staff and creating a strategy around this valuable workforce.

→ A salon that has a creche for busy moms and has all the necessary paperwork in place can create a campaign around this service.

Setting yourself apart from others and meeting the demands of clients and staff allows you to generate a strong growth strategy. The key is to have the time and headspace to think and execute such drastic actions. Remember that your idea might not align with the needs of clients or staff, so conducting market research before execution can be impactful in the long run.

Believe in your vision and dream, as it can have great energy. However, remember that flexibility requires more than just a thought process. Support, delegation, and implementation are also important. This is where your leadership skills will grow even further.

Making the Business Work For You

It is always easy to say to work on the business rather than in the business, but it is a lot harder to achieve. This is what we do best while coaching, as we delve into the numbers and details of the operation and build it so that it never relies on you alone.

There is a huge sense of guilt when it comes to working as and when you want in your business. I'm not sure if it's an industry thing or not, but since you have managed and worked through blood, sweat, and tears, it can become difficult to think of how you will ever take a step back from it all.

Again, it's all about how the business can work for you rather than against you, and for that, there are three S's to consider (I think you must have had the gist of it from this book!):

→ Structure

→ Systems

→ Strict follow-ups

You can take a step back if you are organized in your structure, have created systems that suit your business, and have strict follow-ups to ensure everyone knows what is expected of them and keeps growing themselves.

Making the business work for you is the best thing you could do for yourself as an entrepreneur, and here is an example of what I am working on with my members:

→ Monday and Tuesday: Admin for figures, HR, procedures, management, and any meetings

→ Wednesday: Marketing and networking

→ Thursday and Friday: As you wish! Off, working with clients, working on your project, whatever takes your fancy or is needed at the time

Why not? If you pay staff members to be more involved and develop them in your business, you can reap the benefits of it all. It is something that you can work towards, and if you put your mind to it, you will succeed in the life you truly want.

Work-Life Wellness

I always believe that achieving a work-life balance is difficult, but there are always habits we can adopt to generate one. It's crucial to support your wellness, and since we work in the wellness industry, surely that should be easy, right? However, your wellness, as well as that of your staff, can be costly. Is that why it's so difficult to implement?

Self-care is selfless and should be part of your leadership programme. Again, there is so much pressure in doing it the right way, but what is the right way? "Make what makes you happy," I read somewhere. Sometimes it's hard to even know what makes you tick when you are bogged down with everyone else's needs and wants, including the day-to-day operation of your business.

Work-life wellness is essential to fit into your weekly routine, and here is that word again, routine! Doing something that inspires you and makes you focused is vital. Revisit your time management to make that happen. If you're unsure of what inspires you, then give yourself selfless time. Take a couple of hours to just wander and feel the day-to-day hustle and bustle of your city/town. Drive to a nearby happy place, and that alone is meditation.

But whatever happens, that time is yours, and sometimes just giving yourself the gift of just being is enough. Too often, we are just too busy to get things right in our business. Throughout that process and more, taking a step back for self-care is perhaps the most important aspect of change. That change will take place when making space in your routine to prioritize yourself. When your lifestyle prioritizes you, you will find that you become a better leader for yourself and ultimately others, and that, in itself, makes your business grow.

7
LEAD THE WAY

Your Leadership Plan

Now it is time for you to take a step back and revisit your Seven Steps of Leadership.

Take a big piece of paper and write down the seven steps and start analysing:

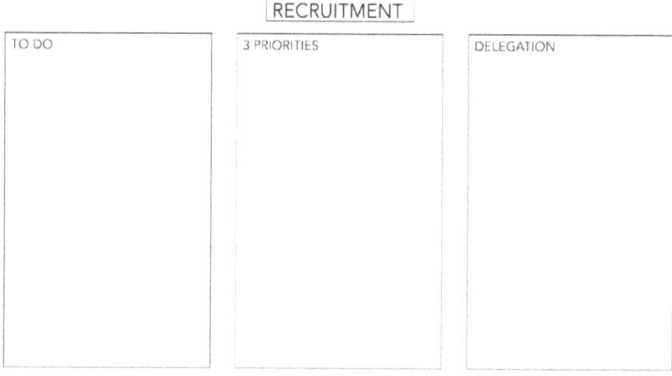

Design your recruitment procedure and ensure that you have the priorities set for recruitment, the more organised you are the more efficient you will become at recruitment, cutting off the time wasters and showing your business as organised and engaging from the start.

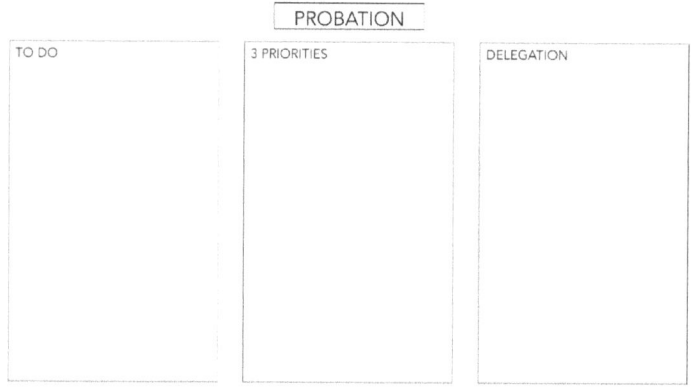

Remember that first impressions count and the consistency of your probation period, meetings, training, and focus on the new team member is the best way to engage them for the long term and to ensure that you have done everything in your power to set them up for success.

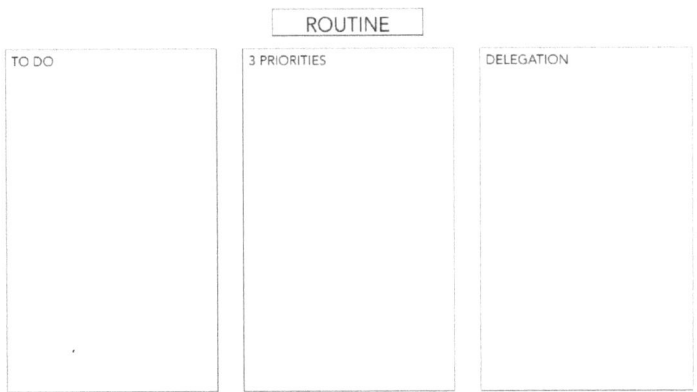

When it comes to establishing a routine, it's crucial to have a plan for each individual and to monitor their progress with an individual development plan. Focus on what impacts each person's personality to continue to empower them daily. Ensure your time management is on point to grow the business, so revisit that aspect if it's not your strong suit.

It's all about follow-ups with your individual meetings. They should be in the diary for the year ahead. Also, start thinking about a delegation strategy to grow the individual skills so that the systems rely on systems rather than one person.

With your management team, ensure your weekly meetings are impactful with key agendas and follow-up on any actions you have defined with them.

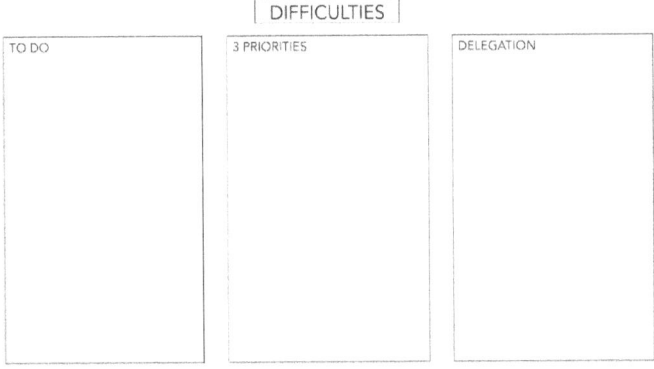

Do you face any challenges within your team? Do you have appropriate procedures and HR support in place if needed? Implement these procedures through your Standard Operating Procedure (SOP) manual and begin with the most crucial ones first. Evaluate the challenges you currently encounter in all areas of the business. Is it your structure that is working against you? Make changes to foster business growth.

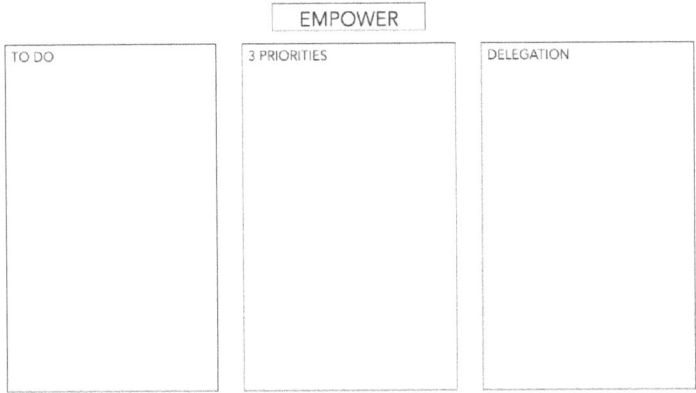

Empowerment starts with your monthly team meeting and yearly team building, as well as understanding what each team member wants to achieve personally. It is important to revisit what isn't working, such as commission and incentives. Think outside the box to create an incredible energy on a daily basis.

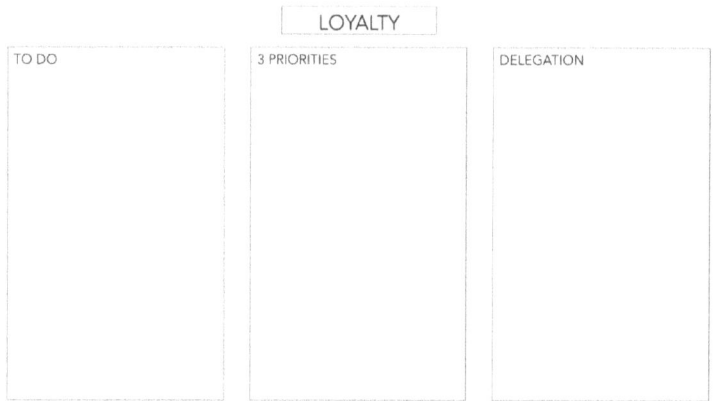

How can you generate loyalty within your business? This is through training for the long term. Start thinking about individual strengths, wants, and needs and build on that to generate long-term engagement. Would it be through a different commission structure? Does your budget need revisiting to generate a win-win situation for your staff?

Now, take your timeline/planner for the year ahead and focus on what you can do and when. It is crucial that you revisit the focus on priorities to ensure you are growing each area of your staff's journey and continuing to empower your teams.

Individual Development Plan & Staff Wellness Formula

➜ INDIVIDUAL DEVELOPMENT PLAN

I strongly believe that people thrive when you focus on their inner strength. What's the point of making someone try to achieve a target that you know they'll find hard to reach and won't empower them? What's the point of working towards something that's unreachable?

I think this applies whether you're working alone or with a team. A target can be fun and empowering, but if it becomes a drag or something that's just given for the sake of it, then what's the point?

I remember an owner telling me that she had gone to a retail training with a trainer who told them that they should be targeting £2,000 per month in retail sales for each staff member. However, some were achieving £300 or less. What's the point? The owner said, "Well, they had the training, now they should achieve it?!"

Really? Is the training so strong that it will make them achieve an extra £1,800 per month overnight? If someone is incapable of selling and just gets lucky with sales, it's beyond teaching them a sales technique. It's about following them, encouraging them, and guiding them through a process rather than expecting them to suddenly become good at something.

I once had a therapist who was the worst at selling. She was perhaps selling £100 per month, which was minor, especially when you expect £1,000 or more per month. Every time she saw me, she shook in fear because she was worried I would ask her questions about her sales. I scheduled meetings with her and told her I was going to take her through a process, and I was sure she would enjoy retail sales afterward.

The process was simple: let's talk about you selling one product a week, that's four a month, rather than giving you a money target. It never mattered about the money generated, just one product a week. She was seeing 50 people that week, that should happen. She was encouraged every time she sold something, asked about the process of what she did for bigger sales, and encouraged to talk the managers through it. She was focused. After four weeks, I asked for two products a week, then three, then four, then one a day. It took six months. In the meantime, she listened to sales techniques on YouTube, started using some of them, and became the highest earner in commission through retail sales. She started enjoying it and understood what I wanted to do.

As a leader, retail sales are important, so my team knows that it will be part of their roles. It can be fun and empowering, but the minute it becomes boring and "a must", the team tends to go against it. Revisiting your way of doing things according to your team is so important, and for that, your yearly individual plans become your focus on their growth.

Dissecting the target into small bite-sized chunks and going through everything with her, including my way of selling, triggered trust and fun around it rather than dread and scarcity.

I love having a folder with everything to do with that staff member, from training to HR, all in one place to follow their journey with you. The key is that if the managers deliver weekly or monthly meetings and the owner does a quarterly meeting, all of the notes are kept in this folder, there is never any back-and-forth communication. It's all very clear. The individual also feels followed and taken seriously.

I met with an owner who asked me, "Why should I invest in my staff member when I feel she is going to leave after six months?" Firstly, if the processes are in place, you can carefully plan when to train her on what, and secondly, can you afford not to invest in your staff? Should you create a business based on fear of people leaving, or should you empower them to become leaders themselves and be a part of that growth? We have become too focused on fear rather than empowerment. Yes, there are bad employees out there, but there are also some gems, and it's time to start focusing on what's right rather than what's wrong!

If an individual wants to learn something, focus on that. The more empowered they are, the more your business will be empowered!

→ STAFF WELLNESS FORMULA

A staff wellness formula is all about engaging your staff and providing rewards that go beyond commission-based incentives. Recently, when I reviewed a budget with one of my team members, she suggested putting money aside each month for the year ahead so that she could give each of our staff members a month's salary as a year-end bonus. Brilliant!

Focusing on your team is key to engaging them for the long term.

Create a staff journey inclusive of your Staff Wellness Formula.

When creating your staff journey, it's crucial to include your Staff Wellness Formula. Make sure to highlight all the things you do for your staff, as you may be doing more than you realize! To help your staff truly value these offerings, create a poster that outlines and emphasizes what you're providing.

It's All About Follow-Ups

I want to emphasize this so much that it has to have its own chapter. Without making your team a priority, you will fail at many aspects of your growth. Following up on things that you do takes discipline and an understanding that it is the most important aspect of your growth. Following up requires organizational skills and systems put in place so you are constantly on top of your following up.

For example, there is no way you would see me doing a stocktake after a while. No time for it, done it for so many years, time to develop someone else to do that. I would train a couple of people, and from there on, I would let them get on with it. However, I would follow up. The team would think I would do this sporadically and unannounced, but it was always in my diary when to do this follow up. Twice a month, I would block a couple of hours to print the stock and do random spot checks. If what is in the system is the same as what is on the shelves, all good. If it said we had four of this item but could only see three, I would make whomever responsible for the stock recount that particular range. I would do that for 20 SKUs (stock keeping units) so I would get a general feel of how the stocktake is going. I would always get them to recount the range in question as otherwise, how would they learn if I did it? Giving responsibilities and ensuring that they know what needs to be worked on is the only way to grow others and develop their skills.

Follow-ups, follow-ups, follow-ups. I want to emphasize that so much that everything you do, everything you ask for MUST have an automatic thought process: When can I follow this up, let me put it in my diary right now.

It is crucial that you make it a priority at that time; otherwise, you send the message that it's never important enough to warrant a follow-up. That brings disgruntlement to your team and ultimately yourself: I should have, I could have, I would have.

Micromanagement is reinforcing your habits, and unless you make change a priority, it will always be the same, and you will always feel on that wheel.

Confession Time!

Marie had taken it upon herself to change the commission structure she had in place because she felt it was necessary to motivate her team. Unfortunately, Marie never checked with her team and announced it in a team meeting, making everyone feel extremely nervous and afraid to voice their concerns. Marie was deflated, feeling that she was doing everything in her power to empower her team, but she completely dismissed engaging them prior to this process, and instead completely destabilized their livelihood. When we discussed the commission, I told her that although they could earn more money, it was complicated to understand, and therefore, the way it was introduced would have been better in a one-to-one meeting, and then reinforced the message in a team meeting.

In the long term, the commission never worked. Being too complicated, Marie ended up going back to the old commission. The team felt unstable and devalued, even if they could earn more money. They were unable to respond to something that was viewed as being forced upon them.

The Leader Inside You - A Recap of What's Next

Quick fire round of questions...

What do we need in place for Leadership to happen?

Foundations of the business through solid procedure

What's the most important when it comes to Leadership?

Structure of your team

What is the fuel of Leadership?

Love of people

What is the effect of Leadership?

Achievement of your vision

What makes us a great leader?

Knowing how to empower our teams

. . .

Why is Leadership difficult?

Because we are dealing with emotions

Why is Leadership a skill?

Because we learn to adapt to situations

Why Leadership questionable?

Because you do not believe in your Leadership skills

Why is Leadership not happening?

Because there are no consequences for actions or non-actions

Why is Leadership not clear?

Because you haven't developed your soft skills

How do I make my Leadership strong?

Keep learning about Leadership

. . .

How do I empower others?

Acceptance of different personalities

How do I achieve my lead my team forward?

Clear, detailed and communicated vision

How is my Leadership perceived?

Through clear communication (team and individual meetings)

How can we become a great leader?

Exceeding expectations

Who is it affecting?

My personal and professional life

Who is benefiting?

My customer journey

. . .

Who learns from it?

My managers and I

Who is supporting that Leadership?

My dream team

Who creates Leaders?

Leaders create Leaders

EPILOGUE

1
FINAL REFLECTIONS

When it comes to micromanagement, it is easy to revert back to your old ways. Micromanagement is reassuring and comforting. The more you control, the more satisfied you feel with the fact that you know what is happening and your ego is fed. Ego is mainly the main ingredient that comes over your mind and peppers doubts, but mainly wants you to stay in your own lane. Coming out of your comfort zone is constantly pushed back, so it takes a huge amount of effort and mindset to change those habits and move forward towards leadership. Ultimately, micromanagement is difficult to break since, as soon as something goes wrong when you try and let go to trust the process, it reinforces that your old ways are better, more precise, and concise. I also find that there is such a fine line between your personal and professional life, and when you go through tough times, the need to control something that you can control (usually work) can reassure and give you a sense of purpose.

So, what should you focus on?

→ Alignment: Are you currently aligned with your business? Are your values and ethos aligned with both your business and personal life? As you have read, running an operational business can make it difficult to stay focused on the bigger picture and grow towards what you truly want. We see it again and again in our one-to-one coaching sessions where it can be overwhelming and discouraging. However, being aligned with who you are and what you do is the most important aspect of your leadership. When you are aligned, everything becomes smoother, and you create a path towards your view of success.

→ Everyone Matters: Everyone has a place in your business, whether they are the GM or the junior staff. Understanding the value of each staff member is key to creating a strong sense of unity. However, having consequences for actions or inactions is the only way to create a structure that aligns with your values. It allows you to create a strong sense of structure where everyone understands your values, and as far as I am concerned, allows you to create a business where everyone can be led to becoming the leader of what they want to achieve themselves. By giving the freedom to become who each wants to be developed in, you empower each of them with the guidance you believe in. That's true leadership. When someone leaves, it becomes a wonderful story of their growth that makes you proud of their achievement and ultimately yours. The leader has zero ego.

→ Headspace: To lead effectively, you must give yourself enough headspace and time to revisit your path. Day-to-day things can happen that will test your leadership skills, and taking time to assess and reassess everything that happened to realign yourself is key to growing your business. It is essential to plan ahead, so you can keep realigning yourself and create that pathway. Taking time out, whether it be a day a week, a business retreat (check out our yearly retreat on our website), and generating that time management to work for you. To empower others, you must empower yourself first. Time out will give you that.

→ Crystal Clear Focus: Everyone I meet that has a crystal clear focus will be quicker at achieving their goals and becoming the leader they want to be. It's easy to fall back in love with your business when you are bogged down with so many personal and business-related things, but it's the only way to create something that makes sense to you. Once the operation is set so that it works for you rather than against you, it becomes easier to find your focus, and that is why I love one-to-one coaching that helps to clarify your path. The clearer you are, the better your communication with others and yourself. The guilt in finding it hard to keep focused is mainly with the fact that you are feeding yourself with far too much information that makes you doubt and change path. Accountability and creation of your Leadership plan will help you create strong growth.

→ Habits: This is the only way to keep focused and create a strong sense of control over what you want to create, rather than trying to control everyone around you. Habits create trust and generate a sense of belonging, which, weirdly, makes you trust yourself in your ability to handle anything that is thrown at you. Start small and grow. You never had to be a carrot-munching yogi, but you have to create habits that align with your values. It's key to become selfless and self-focused. If you believe in yourself, then you have a better chance of people believing in you and wanting to follow you on your path.

Final Reflections

I asked you on Page 48 to assess how you are currently functioning. It is crucial to reflect on your progress. Too often we are very good at highlighting what we are not doing, but it's time you keep writing your wins and your focuses. Work on a quarterly basis and assess to keep growing.

For me, ultimately, leadership is growing others to achieve their best without expecting anything in return but the pleasure of supporting and helping. It is never seen as competition, but as the creation of other leaders. Leadership in your personal and professional life, whether you have a team or work alone, requires soft skills that will allow you to overcome various situations. A micromanager is often scared and feels the need for control, but I find that they are mainly concerned with the outcomes and want to guide every decision to control the result. The more you try to control the outcome, the more you feel in control. A true leader will never be scared and is prepared to fail or win. That's the key difference between the two.

In summary, leadership is a skill that can be taught, but your ability to take a step back, trust, and observe a situation, whether it be personal or professional, is something only you can do. Wanting to change for the better is the only way to change. Changing habits is hard, but you can start by analyzing your leadership and focusing on your time management.

That's why we have created our business around key aspects of support, and our sole mission is to empower as many business owners as we can through:

→ A specific course to complement this book including all of the downloads and further your Leadership skills

→ Nine programs for owners with teams and owners without teams

→ Inside Chat Subscription on Facebook for £55 a month, which is a community of like-minded owners to build support and create a sense of belonging

→ YouTube channel to listen to our values and ethos, answer questions that are sent to us, and give you a boost in supporting you

→ Workshops - simply connect to our monthly newsletter to stay informed

→ Visit our site: www.thedelforgegroup.co.uk

→ Contact us at support@thedelforgegroup.co.uk for anything you might have.

. . .

Final Reflections

And do send us a review on online - we do love a review! How did this book make you feel??

I believe that we are all leaders, and in an operational business, the more you structure, the better, so your leadership can flow. In all, leadership of your team, your life, and your business is crucial to keep loving yourself and loving others. Even if you work with a small team, on your own, or a larger team, your mindset, habits, and focus are the most important. Setting yourself apart from your competitors is beyond shouting about how amazing you are. In any case, that's just showing off and could be seen as too self-centered, which would have the opposite effect of leadership.

Leadership is believing in who you are, what you do, and creating a strong sense of direction to lead your energy and business towards it. Zero strategy means zero leadership. Drum your drum and believe in yourself, and you will start attracting what you deserve.

ABOUT THE AUTHOR

With her wealth of knowledge and expertise, coupled with her passion and extraordinary ability for coaching, Valerie Delforge set up as an International Business Strategy Consultant in 2013. Her mission is to share everything she has learned along the way and lead entrepreneurs, owners, and CEOs on a path to success by empowering them to take their businesses to the next level.

Valerie then created her online training hub, The Delforge Group®. Through a unique combination of one-to-one coaching, online training modules, retail training for teams and managers, management and reception group coaching, recruitment, and HR support, The Delforge Group® will help you increase your profitability and cashflow, as well as empower you to achieve your dreams.

Valerie's impressive CV includes experience with a range of luxury beauty brands and as the Head of Spa

Operation for a large corporation before setting up as a consultant in 2013. As a consultant, Valerie supports entrepreneurs in the service industry to grow their businesses and create a strong foundation for year-on-year success.

www.ingramcontent.com/pod-product-compliance
Lightning Source LLC
Chambersburg PA
CBHW040243130526
44591CB00039B/2793